UNLUCKY IN

LOVE

CONFESSIONS OF A DIE HARD ROMANTIC

By

ORLENA CAIN

Make Your Own Luck in Love

Love Orlena

Table of Contents

FOREWORD

Connection is a powerful word. It's defined by Webster's as; *a relationship in which a person, thing, or idea is linked or associated with something else.* Have you ever met someone and knew you would instantly be friends? Have you had that instant 'connection?' I had that moment when I met the beautiful Orlena Cain. I instantly knew she was as damaged as I was, but that she had the power to forgive, an ability that I do not possess.

Abuse affects everyone differently; there is no doubt the effects last a lifetime, and some amazing people have the power to forgive their abusers in their pursuit to live a better life. Not for their abuser's sake, but for their own. Orlena is one such amazing person. Orlena loves so deeply. She puts her entire heart and soul into every relationship, but she is scared. She is scared of being hurt, and rightfully so. How many times can one person be hurt and still possess hope for a better outcome on the next try? I have been witness to Orlena's many attempts at love, even when I knew deep in my soul that it was wrong and would not work, I supported her because that is what a true friend does. I stood in witness to a marriage I knew was doomed. I was the only person who expressed to her that it was doomed, because I loved her, and still do.

Reading this book, I knew how exposed Orlena was making herself. Is there a more beautiful representation of a person then choosing to bare one's soul for the entire world to read? Kudos to my dear friend for having the guts to be honest enough with herself and with her audience on such sensitive topics. I have been blessed to share a long friendship with Orlena, and I know that I speak for all that call her a friend when I say that we so hope the right person will come along soon, because she deserves it. She deserves to be loved, to be in love, and to know the joy of loving someone that has her back in every situation. To your amazingly bright future, my dear friend, I will always have your back.

~Dr. M. Jill Sporidis~

Orlena Cain is an established Canadian radio and TV personality with over 15 years of celebrated presence in the industry. She has recently delved into further developing her writing talents with a background in journalism.

In this candid memoir, she tactfully shares her tumultuous journey to find love and happiness in a bid to inspire others to discover the importance of healing and self-love in the wake of trauma.

A Note from the Author

No one experience can or should define who you are for the rest of your life. It's the layers of experiences that allow you to grow and shape who you want to become, in love and life. It is my vision that this story will help shed the shame so many women experience on the journey to self-discovery.

Orlena

ACKNOWLEDGEMENTS

To my beautiful and loving good friend Janine Gothard who always encouraged me to write a book. She would always say that I have lived so many lives and had so many experiences, that I really need to share them with the world.

To my strong and loving good friend Jill Sporidis, who devoted her time and energy into editing this book and always believed in me and loved me.

Thank you ladies. You both have such beautiful relationships with your husbands and I hope to find one just like them one day.

I wish to express an extra special thank you to Darek Wierzbicki, Studio 237 for doing such a wonderful job with my hair and to Linda Raddan for doing my makeup for the book cover.

Prologue

Although it may seem silly to begin with a prologue about where I'm at in my life now in a memoir, I felt it necessary to reveal how my story progresses from my early life experiences until today. Through the course of my life, I've treated every relationship as a valuable lesson. I've tried to walk away with something tangible to help shape me into a better version of who I already was.

Until recently, I never had a complete understanding of why I found true love so elusive. The answer to why I kept repeating the same patterns in choices for partners never occurred to me. Neither did the details of what always lead to the inevitable end of those relationships.

One goal I have with my story, is to reach others who struggle with the effects of past trauma. My hope is to shed the shame so many people feel about failed relationships, and being victimized. It is nearly impossible to release the guilt and shame victims carry in their hearts and souls. It has become a daily mantra for me.

Some of my journey may seem a little sporadic to you. Ideally, a memoir should be in chronological order for the events the author recounts. My thinking, as I wrote, was to characterize similar personalities of people in my life with chapter titles that are generic and non-identifying. That's the way I sort them out for myself. My

Lucky in Love

editor reflected to me, areas of my unresolved trauma showed in my writing, as I tend to pen those accounts in present tense.

As for where I am at now, once you've read the entire story, you'll see for yourself.

.

Chapter 1: THE BEGINNING

How do I confess to be a die-hard romantic when I have had so many failed relationships? Wouldn't that make me a failure at love? No matter how many failed relationships and romances I've had, I've never given up on the idea of love. Hey, you can't speak logic to a delusional romantic sometimes. Having had the odds stacked against me and my ideas of love since the beginning of my life, it's even more of a miracle that I even care about love. I have come to learn that love consists of many ideas and concepts, and that the ideas of romance that we are given in books and movies are not 100 per cent accurate to what real life actually is.

Although I never really looked for a fairytale, I thought that real love was a more perfect feeling than it really is. I never grew up reading fairytales, and so the fact that I have bought into their existence is strange. In fact, my childhood was anything but a fairytale. Perhaps fairytale stories resonated within me because they were an escape from my childhood nightmare, which consisted of living with the villain of a fairytale. The nightmare of my childhood didn't hamper my ability to dream of the prince who would rescue me from my life and set free my heart that had been imprisoned by the villain.

As each year slipped by in my youth, the idea that someone

would come along who would love me for me became more and more of a dream. The more damage and pain I endured, the more futile I thought it would be for a prince of sorts to find me. Later in life, I hoped for a man that would not be afraid of the independence that I had developed as I moved through my life of perpetual struggles. I hoped for a man who would see all that I had been through in my life and love me in spite of it. I hoped for someone who would see that I was courageous enough to keep trying despite my inability to allow myself to feel real love. I tried so many times and failed, but I never gave up.

Yes, it may have appeared that I failed to some, but there were lessons learned in each encounter and I will share what those were throughout this book. I always thought that one day I would find that someone who would understand me despite my losses and be the one to fight the villain in my fairytale and win my hand.

Why does a relationship that feels so right always end? I believe that you learn through your relationships what you don't want, but that you eventually get what you need. It's difficult in today's world where we are cultivated to be strong and independent women, to find someone who is truly comfortable with that concept. It seems that the more competent you are, the less tolerant of bullshit you become. Who needs to step up their game then? Or should women tone down their game? Be less than they are? I don't think so. I have always been intolerant of fake crap. I call a spade a spade and I don't see the purpose in overlooking bullshit as I believe it will always come back to you in a negative and hurtful way if you do. So, I call it, move on from it, and find something better suited for me.

I am a self-made woman. I have learned from my mistakes and hurts and I always trudge on like a soldier of love. I remember the day

I heard the singer Sade sing the song, "Soldier of Love," and it resonated with me and what I felt about who I was in this world.

So, who or what is the villain in my life? It's different for every person, but for me, three integral men in my life set me on the run from love. I never grew tired of running and I was always confident in knowing I was too fast to be caught. My father, my stepfather, and my grandfather are the three men who have failed me in their examples of how and what a man should be for a woman.

My father was a womanizer who had two children in one year with two different women, one of which was me. My mother was fifteen when she met my father who was significantly older. Why would a fifteen year old be with an older man? Because, her father, my grandfather, was an alcoholic, and never was a good example of what a man should be, neither to his wife or his children.

The instinct to run from those who you fear became instilled in me when my mom ran from my father. However, when you run, you often don't know where you are running to and are merely running from something. My father ran too. He ran to the other woman he had a baby with the same year I was born. The other woman had a son and so he married her. Yes, back then, his family wanted the legacy of the name carried on. Therefore the boy was more valuable to the family. Despite his choices, he continued an affair with my mother while married to the other woman until I was four-years-old. That was the last I saw of him until much later in life. I saw a photo of him when he remarried yet another woman. I was a tween and never gave much thought to where he was, but always had hoped he would come back and save me.

So my young mother was left single and alone with a child in the seventies, much like a sitting duck in the world. Damaged from her own childhood, my mother was the perfect victim for my stepfather. He was a pedophile, an abusive man who infected our lives for the next ten years. This is where the villain entered my story that did the most damage in my life and instilled the most fear in me. This man is the reason that I ran from every idea that had to do with love and relationships, because of how wrong everything he taught me was.

Then began my pattern of running from every man I connected emotionally with. I ran away from relationships so much so that I could have been called the 'Runaway Girlfriend.' Call the movie directors; move over Julia Roberts, your Runaway Bride movie was over in less than ninety minutes. Mine would be a syndicated, long-running television series consisting of torrid love affairs, fast and fleeting romances, and trysts that would only ever be just that. Ships passing in the night with promises and lies of love; I have experienced it all. Young love, first love, foolish love, doomed love, and bad love, all of which materialized into my life in one way or another. But, for some reason, I never gave up. I was convinced at the end of every single relationship that it wasn't the one. I also believed at the very beginning of the next relationship that it could be the one. Well, I used to think that way.

In one relationship story I share, I'll refer to myself as Rapunzel. I let down my hair to someone I perceived as a Prince, he climbed up and made me fall in love with him, then promptly slid down my hair, cut it all off, and left me heartbroken. His aim was to prevent any other Prince from ever being able to climb up it and win my heart. I sat in disbelief and thought, *How could you do that to me? How could you make promises, make me swoon, make me dream of love and then in a swift argument, demand my engagement ring back and bam, it's over?* I will share this story of the prince who became a jester to me in much further detail in this book; the prince who was referred to by my friends as the boyfriend in a box; the one who came complete with children, debt, a dog, and a not-so-nice-ex-wife.

Before I get to all the stories and lessons in love, I have to go back to when I was a young girl in public school, where boys did not like me, "in that way." This was ok with me, because I didn't like them in that way either, nor did I ever pursue boys in the way other girls did.

In public school, I did like some boys, sure I did, but I had so many things going on in my life at home that I never felt comfortable with the idea of having a boy around me in that intimate close way. I never actually had a boyfriend until high school, mostly because I wasn't allowed to. I also never had friends come to my house. No one was allowed to call me on the phone and I wasn't allowed to go to anyone else's house either. That made it difficult to connect to anyone in life. I was pretty intolerant of the usual shenanigans that boys get up to in public school. I developed a reputation that people shouldn't mess with me unless they wanted the stuffing kicked out of them. I had no fear because I was getting beaten by a grown man at home. Taking on a kid my own age didn't scare me in the least and I made sure it was known to everyone.

Despite all that was going on at home, I excelled in school. Regardless of what you may think about kids who are severely abused, not all of them do poorly in school. I was an incredible student and even a great athlete. I lived in a parallel world, where at school, I was safe, and I was in control of what was going on there. I was, however, under strict discipline at home and when it came to my studies, I was pushed hard even before I went to school for kindergarten. My stepfather was hard core about my education and how well I did or didn't do was a reflection on him.

Yet he was not a bright man at all. I remember one night not being able to spell a word properly and long before Google existed, I was forced to sit at the table until ten o'clock at night, dumbfounded and unable to come up with an adequate response. My mother finally rescued me and that would be one of the only two times she ever did, by whispering the response to me when the villain wasn't looking. That was just one of many times he was overly aggressive with my learning and education. As big and powerful as the villain was, he was a coward, a thief, and an abusive man. I surpassed his intelligence by the end of public school.

But I digress; now back to the boys, or lack thereof. In grades seven and eight, I was allowed to go to the school dances, but that wouldn't help me get a boyfriend. I didn't really want one at that time. Even though all the other girls seemed to be getting one. All the developing girls were the attraction to the young boys at school, but not me. I was a flat-chested athlete who did well academically and had spent most of my public school days focused on sports and my friends.

When it came time that I should be interested in them, none were really interested in me. I remember having one or two boyfriends for a short period of time. When I let it slip at home that I did have one, I had to say good-bye. One boy from public school I had as a boyfriend and that lasted for less than a few hours. By the time I got home and had dinner, I had to call him and tell him I couldn't be his girlfriend. That was an awkward conversation and extremely brief.

It wasn't like I was in the best place in my life to even consider a boyfriend anyway. My world at home was volatile and I had to summon every ounce of strength in me to endure the hours until I left for school the next day. I loved waiting for the bus every morning and anticipated the ride with excitement. I hated Fridays as I knew that I would be alone all weekend with the villain when my mother wasn't home. I would even ask the school bus driver to drive slower on Fridays.

Young love and romance evaded me. The relationship wiring that happens in us from learned experiences and examples at home, was a complete mess inside me. My emotional construction was like a subway map of New York City; all over the place and hard to decipher, like spaghetti on a plate. Just when I felt the wiring of emotions went one way, something would happen. Confusion took hold of me and my emotions rerouted themselves. Sort of like an electrical current that jumps a circuit. I could never seem to get ahead of it.

My emotional chaos kept me timid around boys, and although I had crushes and I had the desire to be interested in them, I just couldn't make sense of the intricate workings of it all. I had only experienced two minor kisses from boys. One of which was at summer camp where I met a really sweet boy who was kind to me the whole time I was there and wanted to kiss me. One night after dinner and prayer (it was a church camp, because all the best things happen at church camp), we agreed to meet in the forest that divided the two camp sites.

The boys were stationed way up on a hill and the girls were closer to the water. The only way to the boy's camp site was through the forest. I was only twelve and it was one of those moments you don't forget. Although I can't remember his face, his nickname was Bertie. It was sunset and we only had a small window of time to spend before any counselors began their nightly checks and count. It began with a tender embrace. He wrapped his arms around me, then pulled me in close and planted a kiss on my lips as we heard the echo of voices through the trees. He hugged me tight one last time and I ran back to the campsite.

We left the next day, so that was the last time I ever saw him. The second boy who kissed me was someone I had a crush on at school right near the end of grade eight. We met at our school one weekend in the afternoon. It was an impromptu kiss and more formal rather than romantic. I clearly remember he did cut my lip with his braces. Not that I cared though. I felt awkward around boys and was not sure how to switch from looking at them like brothers and schoolmates to possible boyfriends.

Regardless, it was better in the end that I had no real boyfriends. The truth was, my stepfather was grooming me and abusing me to be his obedient servant. Night and day, I was at his beck and call. Whatever he wanted, whenever he wanted it. He was a horrible person. He became the villain in my life who left a wake of fire and devastation in my fairytale before it ever began. The villain was never at rest in my life and I was his obsession and object to own and torture. I feared him, but he and others in the family made me tell him I loved him. I didn't. I hated him. He tainted my experiences and emotions with his poison, robbed me of a childhood, and stole my virginity. Yes, when I was the tender age of twelve, he took the only possession I could call my own and what was left of my innocence. He even forced my mother to make me take birth control. I wasn't sexually active with boys. Why at the age of twelve would I be forced to take birth control? Why didn't anyone question him about that?

When I turned thirteen, my mother finally left my abusive stepfather and this actually sent my whole life into a tail spin. It was too little too late. The damage had been done. Without him dominating my life and every move, my shackles and chains fell off and like a dog that had been chained up its whole life, I ran free. I instantly rebuked anyone and everyone who tried to tell me what to do. The summer before my grade nine school year was spent on the run. Part of the guidelines of the separation between my mother and stepfather was that my sister and I had to visit him every other weekend. I complied for the first little while. Eventually, I gained the strength as high school started to just take off away from home any weekend I was supposed to go to visit the villain. I do explain this later in the book.

That final Friday came and my mother waited for me to come home from school. I didn't go home. Instead, I hid out at the homes of strangers that were barely friends. I even slept in the forest one time with nothing but my school clothes and jacket on. No one knew why I became so wild and disobedient in my behavior. Family members long suspected abuse, but had no idea the extent of it.

Only a few of my close friends knew I had been severely abused, but I never revealed the details and was too ashamed to speak up. I didn't know how to tell anyone. I was so confused about what happened, and I was so silent for so long. I had gotten used to keeping this secret and I continued to keep silent. My rage grew inside. I exceeded my tolerance for abuse by the age of fourteen. I was tapped out from taking on so much bullshit in my life that I could feel myself cracking inside.

It was only a matter of time, before I would blow up. The villain knew he was losing control. He went to great lengths to try and bribe me and guilt me into not saying anything. Like most abusers do to their prey, he told me no one would believe me. He told me I participated in the abuse, therefore I must have wanted it. I never wanted it and he haunted every one of my romantic experiences long into my twenties. I couldn't have sex with anyone for the longest time without thinking of him. He crept into my thoughts and managed to ruin the most romantic connections I tried to make.

Despite this traumatic experience, the person who broke my heart for the first time was not the villain. It was my mother. She broke my heart when it was all said and done. When we finally left, she didn't even come to my rescue then. She met someone else and he helped her escape the villain, but the person who truly needed her to be brave and leave was me. For so many years, I suffered abuse from the villain and she neglected me. Can you imagine living in a house with adults and everyone matters, but the child? It never made sense to me and I assumed I was a bad kid. No matter what I did to make everyone in the house happy, it was never enough and I still live my life that way. With the feeling that it's never enough. It's impossible to live life never knowing if what you have done is enough, so you keep doing more to please people.

While we were living under the reign of the villain's madness, I always felt she was a victim too. Even though, so many times she would take my sister to town on errands and leave me behind. She could have fought to take me too, but she didn't and she never fought for me at the end either. After the charges were filed against the villain, she never went to court with me. He had over thirteen charges against him for what he did to me. I faced the villain at the time with my foster family, but my own mother never came to court. It was so difficult to face that on my own. All she could do is blame me for being wild and angry.

Some boys I went to school with were in court during the brutally descriptive details. Back then it was an open courtroom and you can only imagine the shame I felt when I saw them sitting in court behind the villain while I had to testify. It was even worse to see them in school afterward. My mother never went to therapy with me either. I was considered a troubled youth and too unmanageable for her to bother with. She didn't want me to live with her anymore either. I always thought that if the villain wasn't around, she would be strong. As it turned out, she still wasn't. I was.

From that moment on I knew that she and I would never be mother and daughter no matter how hard I cried. She would never fight to help save me. When I was placed in foster care, she agreed to sign me away and make me a ward of the court. No mother, no father, I simply belonged to the Government.

After all I endured, this was how I was paid back for my suffering. I took all of that anguish and torture only to be abandoned in the end? My conclusion was that she never wanted me from conception or birth anyway. I was to be adopted. At the hospital, when I was born and when my Oma saw me, (my mother's mother,) she wouldn't hear of having me sent away. She cancelled the plan for adoption. I was to be cared for by relatives and see what would happen after that. As a result of my mother's failure to protect me, my Oma always carried such guilt around. The first four years of my life I was bounced around to my aunts and even my Oma's best friend and husband considered adopting me. But, that wasn't meant to be.

You see, in my Oma's bid to help me as a baby, not only did she cancel my adoption, but in order to give me a proper family, she introduced my mother to a man she saw as a viable father figure. How could she have possibly known he would become the villain in my life story?

As horrific as it sounds, I recognize the difference between my devoted Oma and my mother. Oma spent her life loving me, caring for me and always trying to be there to make up for that. My mother never attempted to make up for anything with me. My mother didn't want me to begin with, and her feelings never changed throughout our lives. I tried for years through my teens to get over the hurt my mother caused me, but in the end, I decided to end the connection with her and move on with my life. I tell people my parents are dead. My father physically died, but my mother is dead to me. My only salvation in life has been my Oma and my Auntie-Ma (my one Aunt). They both are and have always been like a mother to me through my life. My aunt has always come to bat for me in my life on many occasions. She's a woman I could write an entire book about on unconditional love. I still can't believe she is my mother's sister. She's always stuck up for me and has always treated me like a daughter.

As I shed the skin of who I was and I felt the cool air of freedom all around me, you'd think I would be relieved. I did too, but my soul was bare, my skin felt raw and the world became even scarier. I spent my whole life being groomed and conditioned into obedience. During that time, I hung on tightly to what little I had of myself inside. It's like I hid pieces of myself from the villain so deep inside of my soul. To my surprise, I survived all those years and I feel it has a lot to do with many days spent reading books and daydreaming.

Within my books, I grasped at any thoughts in those books that allowed me to dream. I dreamt of the day I would escape this horrible prison called my life. A life in a house far out in the country, where I was kept away from the world as much as possible, so much so, that when we moved into the city it was like moving into a metropolitan. I'd rarely been allowed to come into the city as a child and had been isolated from my relatives. I only ever attended one birthday party. I had no real idea of how things operated and people were all so different.

Growing up, much of what I learned was from television outside my scholastic studies. I was allowed to watch a half hour, to an hour maximum of television a day. That's when I fell in love with the Montreal Canadiens. I spent that precious TV time watching the sport and getting drawn into the excitement of the game. Everything I learned about relationships came from my abusive home life and it was all wrong. I spent most of my life unraveling the thoughts and relearning how things should really be. My trust level was at an all-time low and I believed no one.

My first year of high school was like walking around without any skin on and feeling vulnerable and incredibly paranoid. High school had some of my biggest and saddest moments. I walked around confused most of the time by what people said and did. Young boys in high school were even crueler than in public school. Plus, I couldn't fight them off like I did when I was younger. When we were kids, before the testosterone kicked into boys as teens, we were all equal strength. So, I used intimidation and strength to keep people away from me. I finally began to develop and I went from being flat as a board to having giant boobs and curves all over the course of one summer. I used to pray every night growing up as a tween to finally start to look like a woman and then my wish came true all at once.

Boys called me fat-ass, although it wasn't really fat at all. I was pretty curvy, and my body at the time could easily be compared to J-Lo now, but it wasn't popular back then. So harsh words further cemented my thoughts and confusion about myself. I wanted to disappear from the world. I hated walking down the hallways to my locker or class, because they taunted me. I developed a thick skin early in life and even though they were boys and physically stronger than me, I still mouthed back and dug deep with my insults. I went for the jugular every time. The wounded child in me didn't allow anyone else to hurt me further.

There were several moments in my earlier life that I actually contemplated suicide. I attempted it once when I was fifteen. It was about a year after my visits ended with the villain and when one of the jerks I dated dumped me. I did again when I was twenty-six. The more I tried to fit in and trust people, the harder I found it. Hope failed me during those dark days. I thought *if this is what freedom holds for me then I don't want to be alive at all.*

Where was this love I had seen in movies? Where was the kindness that I hoped to find outside of my horrible home life? I saw other teenagers dating, holding hands and really liking one another, but I felt cursed to walk amongst them. I felt like something was wrong with me.

Despite the few nice guys that did try and express their kindness, I was so damaged by what had happened to me that I gravitated to those who were no good for me at all. The ten years of extensive abuse had taken its toll and I felt like I was a mirror reflecting to everyone how horrible I felt about myself and how insecure I was.

The agonizing mental and physical daily torture became so common place to me, the times I was able to feel joy at home were few and far between. Constant anxiety and instability turned me into an acutely hyper-aware person. The excessive need to always calculate the mood and moves of another can be exhausting, but entirely necessary to have any kind of peace at all. Hypervigilance is a survival skill abused people develop to predict potential threats around them at all times.

When I think back to all the incredibly horrible things that the villain put me through, I can't begin to imagine how I survived. The restless nights, not knowing when he would creep upon me and wake me up to fulfill his sexual needs. When I grew up in the villain's lair, I never even had my own bedroom until I was twelve. From the age of four to twelve, I slept in a four-foot hallway on a mattress that I would lean back up against the wall every morning after I would strip the bedding and fold it.

When I finally got a bedroom, he crept into my room when my mother was asleep and I woke up to his vile and disgusting touch. The things he would do to wake me up were horrible. For many years if someone tried to wake me up while I slept, they would be met with swinging arms. For a long time, no one could cuddle with me while I slept. For those who tried to wake me up seductively, I would jolt awake in terror. It was hard for any partners I had to understand. To the few I tried to explain it to, it was extremely embarrassing. It was easier to just end relationships than to get into it with any of them.

It was truly an awful time in my life. I attended therapy every week, talking about my pain over and over again. I lived in two different foster homes before the age of seventeen. I finally gave up the concept of a happy-ever-after with a family due to my own inability to fully trust people and listen to rules and obey them in a home.

When you're suffocated by so many rules in life, you eventually rebel. The reality was, I felt safer alone, but like a double-edged sword, it made me very lonely. Inside I felt isolated, yet I craved love. My mother never loved me, my father never loved me and the villain tried to destroy me. I felt I was better on my own and pushed to live independently at the age of seventeen.

Lucky in Love

By the time I was in grade twelve, I lived with a guardian who was nineteen. This girl I had become friends with was looking for a roommate and I was desperate to find a place to stay. She agreed to let me stay with her and I finished grade thirteen while we lived together. She was very kind and a good friend to me at that time. I needed somewhere to stay, somewhere I felt safe. I did feel safe there where I didn't have to trust anyone, nor did I have to assimilate to a family life. I was simply incapable of doing so. I had so much to deal with that the last thing I wanted to try and do was have a family. I was on my own and I stayed on my own from there on. So began the dating journey and my quest for love.

As I mentioned earlier, initially, I had to go back every other weekend with my sister, who was his biological child. Even she chose eventually to stop seeing him as well. I hated my mother for sending me back. I wasn't even his biological child and everyone knew how badly he would beat me if I ever disobeyed him. I was sent back to him, regardless.

One day, I met a much older boy in school who told me I didn't have to keep going back to his house. I confided in him. I told him what had happened and he was very kind. Eventually, I ran away from my mother.

On a day I was scheduled to go out to the villain's house, I took off from school and hid. I hid from life. I hid from the truth. I hid from myself. I didn't want to go back to school and I didn't want to face my life or the truth of what happened to me. Even then, I still didn't understand the magnitude of what had been taken from me, my innocence and virginity. I was on the lam for a few weeks and my boyfriend at that time, the much older boy, urged me to turn myself into the police. After all, I was only fourteen and he was eighteen.

As a result, the time came when I needed to step forward. I walked into the police station and turned myself in. Can you guess what happened next? It took me by surprise, but that next step of running would be my last for a while. My life exploded. Exhaustion finally took hold, as I had grown tired of running. I couldn't go on the way I was any longer. In spite of all of the villain's malicious conditioning and grooming, I told them everything that had happened to me and why I ran away from home. The arresting officer had to sit down, as the years and years of abuse poured out of my mouth and into his ears.

After it was all said and done, I didn't want to go back home. There was no reason or will inside me to return to the hell I had finally escaped. Instead, I went to an emergency receiving home/foster home. It was one of the first times I actually felt peace. Finally, someone knew what had happened and I could rest. On a side note, that officer kept in touch with me throughout my life and through some very difficult times as I purged the abuse from my soul. Right up until a few months before he passed away, he called me periodically to check in on me.

Eventually I had to go back to school the next semester. Positivity began to enter my life as I won an award for getting back on track and focused on school again. With the good, we still have to navigate through the bad. Intensive therapy was set up to help me work through the trauma. I maintained my visits to a therapist throughout high school. It was good for me, but it was a struggle through the whole thing. Baring your soul after years of abuse leaves you feeling naked and vulnerable, which can be just as scary. They say the truth is supposed to set you free, but it doesn't really. In my experience, that isn't always the case. For me, it caused me to feel more imprisoned

19

than ever. I had to confront everything I'd been through, and with that, I had to face all the emotions that came crashing to the surface. All this while being under the scrutiny of being a teenager. Talk about maximum overload. I was a sitting duck through high school.

Chapter 2: THE JERKS

The Urban Dictionary provides a pretty elaborate meaning for a Jerk. *"The Jerk is the type of guy women usually want when they say they want a nice guy. Jerks are selfish, manipulative bastards who see women as little more than sexual conquests to brag about to their buddies or mere objects that are there for their personal pleasure.*

The rest of the Urban Dictionary speaks to post-sex breakup and how Jerks play the "sensitive guy." It outlines how they manipulate their targets so the girl will make most of the moves on him. After his conquest, he dumps her for some other girl. I found it uncanny that this description also speaks to how he can make it look like she's at fault for coming on too strong, and subsequently she'll take him back if he chooses to return for seconds.

Sounds about right, doesn't it? Sure there are other words to call this type of guy. But a jerk is to the point and boy I have dated some serious jerks. We all have. They're always so memorable. For each one I speak of I will keep it brief, because they really don't deserve a huge amount of acknowledgement. Each one taught me something about myself and life as they always do.

Dumb Jerk

Hmmm, how about the dumb jerk, hockey player who thought he was all that? Every girl wanted this guy and why? Girls wanted him because he was a jerk. He had attitude, bravado, and swagger, as we call it now. Cocky confidence, but nonetheless he was a jerk, and why? In order to get me to date him, he lied about his relationship status and worked an elaborate scheme to get me. I was young, naive and didn't have a lot of self-esteem at this point in my life. Still battered and bruised from my childhood, I fell for every line and believed every word.

It was easy for him to lie, because he wasn't from around here. I was dating someone at that time. Being naive and gullible, I fell for it when he swooned me with words and told me all the things I wanted to hear. I was actually dating a good guy at the time. The good guy I was dating at the time treated me with respect and was incredibly kind and loving. Naturally, the attentive jerk held more appeal to a damaged girl like me. Back then, it never occurred to me that it seemed too good to be true, or maybe the genuine good guy was scarier to my damaged psyche than anything else I had to face.

This guy was determined to prove he wasn't a jerk. I heard he had a girlfriend and confronted him about it. In order to convince me I was wrong, he came to my place and called her. Wow, he called her right in front of me to affirm he was not with her. That's pretty straight up, right? As it turned out, no, he never called his girlfriend. Instead, he called his buddy's girlfriend who played along with the charade so I would go out with him. How gullible I was. I believed the whole elaborate story and no one who knew him told me otherwise.

We went out a few times and even slept together before I finally found out that he did in fact have a girlfriend back home. I lost a nice guy who never forgave me for dumping him for this jerk, and I don't blame him. I apologized much later in life for it, but it was too late, the damage was done.

Teen Jerks

As a teenager, I had more than my share of jerks. When you come of age and have a load of baggage you are toting from your childhood, it makes it hard to have a clear perspective. The way I viewed the world and the people in it, was seriously impaired from the horrible abuse I had experienced from the villain. I literally had no understanding of myself. I was always told what to do and how to do it. I never had my own voice. Ironically, I loved to talk growing up and 1 loved to read. In retrospect, it's no surprise I became a broadcast journalist.

Yet growing up I spent most of my time silent when I was home, nervous about the ominous threat that hovered around me like a menacing storm cloud. When my mother finally left the toxic situation and moved away, I was entering high school. That was even tougher on me. Now I faced the turmoil of moving into the city from living in the country. I went to a new high school full of strangers with none of the friends I grew up with. Not one soul I attended kindergarten to grade eight with would be around to cushion the blow.

Culture shock and more unbearable stress to deal with was my new lot in life. By this point, I didn't even know myself anymore. I walked around most times, uncomfortable in my own skin. When anyone expressed an interest in me or thought I was cute, it came as a shock, but also a relief. For the brief time they liked me, I liked myself.

Throughout high school, I disliked myself most of the time. I stumbled along emotionally. The teenage jerks were everywhere. There were some sweet guys who came into my life, but unfortunately I was far too damaged to feel much of anything. Most are not worth talking about at this point. We were all young, foolish, and let's be honest, never really knew anything at all.

There was, however, one particular guy, even I though can't even remember his name. A transfer student. All the girls in high school were intrigued by him and his friend. Not me. The lack of interest always seems to send a signal to egomaniacs. I spent most of my time in between classes briefly catching up with new friends .In place of today's technology, we actually had to wait to speak to someone after class or in between. On route to class, I had to pass where this one guy's locker was. He wore this intense look that often scared me more than intrigued me.

To keep it brief, I'll explain it like this; he reminded me of a hawk, lurking, leering, and calculating thoughts in his head. I wasn't sure what he was thinking until one day he stared at me long enough that it made me uncomfortable enough to say hello. It was tense and saying hello seemed to breathe air back into the hallway. He said hello back. I walked on. Eventually he would say hello a few more times over the course of a few weeks and I would say hello back but that was all. I heard he had a girl friend of sorts that was on again off again and I never wanted to talk much to him because of that knowledge.

Eventually, he learned my name and even figured out where I

lived. That surprised me when he revealed this information in a brief conversation. He asked for my number once. I said no. When he asked why, I hinted around the fact that he had a girlfriend and he said he didn't anymore that they were on the outs and that talking was no harm. *Okay, sure*, I thought. He would eventually call me a few times, but I never spoke much to him at school or kept track of his whereabouts. When we talked on the phone those few times, he tried to turn the conversation into a sexual one. Not the kinds of conversations you would have at home in ear shot or the kind of way you should be talking as a teenager. His words were quite advanced and so was his behavior. I talked with friends about him calling me and his weird interest in me.

One day I walked to my locker after the end of the day to gather my books. The hallway was vacant and I could see someone at the double doors just past my locker. Even though I had a bad feeling, I proceeded to my locker to get my bag and leave for the day. All of a sudden the door opened up and he came through the doorway toward me with a fierce look on his face that startled me. He walked up to me aggressively and asked if I have told anyone that we were talking? "Of course," I said," I had spoken to a couple of my close friends." "We are only just talking right?"

Apparently he was trying to get his girlfriend back and she heard he'd been calling me. Now I was the one at fault somehow. He grabbed me by my throat and hoisted me against the lockers and said if I didn't keep my mouth shut that he was going to shut it for me. I started crying immediately, I was terrified. He dropped me back onto my feet and rushed away. He didn't return to school the next day and I never saw him again. For that matter, I never asked where he went either. His girlfriend never did say anything to me about the whole situation. I never pursued him at all. He pursued me in a weird way, much like a stalker. It was a lesson I never forgot. This lesson I learned was about what some people are capable of and how dangerous they can be.

Most of my teenage years were filled with empty promises, broken promises and confusion. I didn't understand boys and I couldn't attract a decent guy for the most part. If I did manage to date a nice guy it was always short-lived by my inability to love or be loved. I only knew one thing in connecting with guys, and that was how to give of myself in a physical way. Nothing else. No one taught me the meaning of true intimacy, because the men in my life, the male role models were horrible ones. The villain had managed to damage my ability to understand love and he had shattered my self-esteem and self-worth into a million pieces. I didn't think I was pretty and I was boy conscious from the time I was in high school until I left.

All of my intimate experience was with the villain. He tainted every aspect of my sexuality. The villain used me for his sexual gratification from the time I was four until I was fourteen. When I entered grade nine, he was still abusing me. I couldn't focus on anything and most days I was riddled with anxiety. How could I possibly choose a good guy when I didn't feel good about myself, and I was emotionally unwell? I always felt like I was a short breath away from drowning in my own misery and I would cling to anyone or anything to keep myself from drowning.

Any teeny tiny bit of emotion or interest shown to me by any boy prompted my need to jump all over it. I still feel such sorrow for that time in my life. High school was all about just getting through it and I was angry most times inside, even though I smiled on the outside. I was angry, hurt and incredibly lonely. I just wanted the experience to be over and I desperately wanted to leave Belleville and all the pain behind.

Young love – Hans the Jerk

Everyone has that first boyfriend that you fall head over heels for. The kind of guy who behaves like a gentleman and treats you like a lady. I was pretty young, still a teenager, impressionable and young when I met Hans and he was such a fun guy. He spoiled me, treated me sweetly and we hung out a lot at his house alone. Now when I look back, I think maybe too much in the beginning. He had a lot of freedom from his parents and I had none, I found it great to go to his house.

Where I lived then, he wasn't allowed to come over at all. Most of the time we dated, we just hung out at his place, alone. When two teenagers are left alone for any period of time, things tend to happen. At this time, I still had not quite figured out that sex and love are not the same thing. I had no idea how one felt different from the other. The lines had been so skewed in my head and I couldn't differentiate the two. I fell for Hans a little more every time we slept together. I felt more connected to him and less to the villain.

Then one day, with no forewarning, he dumped me after telling me I was becoming too needy. This was because I loved spending time with him when we were not in school or working. He pulled the old 'I need some space right now' line on me. Space? What did space mean and why did he want space from me if he loved being around me? I was crushed. We had been dating about six months and I really felt something for him, or so I thought. He got the space he wanted from me and I was still confused as to why he needed it in the first

27

place.

Devastated because he wouldn't take my calls, he avoided me at school and pretended like I didn't exist. I was crushed. So much so, that I was at home one day and swallowed a bunch of pills, only to end up in the hospital getting my stomach pumped hours later. It was a horrific ordeal. At the time I was distraught with a broken heart that was barely a heart to begin with. By that point, I was completely shattered.

The week after we split up, we bumped into each other at a party. I thought he was taking his 'space' to go out with his friends. It was a crushing blow to see that he was there with his new love interest. It was at that point I figured out his need for 'space' meant so he could date someone else. It was an unpleasant exchange of words at best. I was a teenager, raging with rejection and not emotionally stable to start with. Our encounter at that party almost ended in a physical altercation between me and the new girl.

Of course I ended up looking like the crazy one because he lied to me and no one likes to be lied to. That's what happens when a guy is dishonest. Guys take note; if you aren't blatantly honest with someone you don't want to be with anymore, or don't give anyone any time to prepare for this inevitable moment; it will end in a negative way. When the rug gets pulled out from underneath you, the insensitive lack of preparation for the emotional turbulence can leave everybody embarrassed.

It also leaves someone wounded. When a woman is wounded it can spark the dire need to get even. Beware the "best friend" hook up guys, because when a woman is really hurt she often realizes she wants nothing to do with you. She may be prepared to sever the idea of ever being with you again. I searched in the phone book and called his good friend to talk about what had happened between Hans and me. It was an opportunity to go watch a movie "as friends," On the way to the movie theatre, as we were about to cross the road, my moment of redemption came.

Hans was driving down the street in his brand new shiny vehicle at the very moment his friend and I walked toward the movie theatre together. Mission completed. Vindication was mine. In hindsight, two wrongs don't make a right. Later, I was able to realize if you hurt the one who hurt you, not only do you waste energy, but you stoop to their level. You become what you despise them to be. It's not a good feeling at all. The bliss of vindication only lasts for a brief moment.

You hope the lessons learned by them are honesty and respect for someone's feelings. Maybe then they will show you the same compassion, maybe that way you can avoid causing them anger after they find out you lied. It may not have been morally the right thing to do on my part, but it sure felt good to see that wince on his face (even for a second) as he gave us both the finger and drove off. No one said the game of love was fair. I never went on another date with his friend and I never talked to Hans again.

My insecurity about my value amplified from that day. Most of the time I became haunted by a constant feeling of insignificance. I used the only thing I felt was worth anything to feel love, and that was sex. Sex seemed to be the thing I knew men wanted from me and because the villain had conditioned me to equate love with sex. I found myself giving that up in order to feel love. It really is a terrible feeling. To give of yourself in the hopes you will feel love only to end up feeling even more empty inside.

In fact, my entire teen years were spent in search of love at any cost. I was so empty inside and felt so worthless. I wasn't picky about who I dated as long as I could feel something like love. Each attempt at finding that elusive goal was short-lived. Like an addict trying to chase that next high, I was frantic to feel love, and to be loved. When you're in a desperate situation at any time in your life that deep-seated need sets off a signal. One that isn't always answered by someone who wants to rescue you. Instead, that urgency tends to draw in someone who wants to take advantage of you.

Teen boys don't usually develop emotional maturity during their youth. This was a fact I came to discover later in life. In my adolescence, my lack of insight left me often broken-hearted. Part of the reason I wanted to leave the city I was raised in, was to leave behind all the pain. I wanted to go and rediscover myself instead of existing in the shell of who I had become. I ran away from who I was conditioned to be, and needed to make a better future for myself.

Bushy Jerk

I spent one summer working in the heart of Yorkville's "*It Spot.*" I just got back from Ireland and decided to take the summer to work. My plan was to save my money to go back to school in September. I needed to be in a spot that was busy nightly and this spot was.it. The who's who visiting included tennis star Andy Roddick, Tori Spelling, Dean McDermott, Paris Hilton and too many others to keep track. I even watched a world cup soccer game one afternoon with some of the staff there alongside Sienna Miller and James Franco. It was that kind of place. There was a lot of development going on in the area and tons of construction workers would come into the restaurant during the day due to the massive patio that was pretty casual in the daytime.

One particular guy, we'll call him Bushy, used to stop in and always wanted me to wait on him. It was no problem, I thought. He always tipped well and was really polite. After a few weeks, he asked if I would like to go for coffee sometime later in the day when he was off work. I thought, *sure why not*. We met a few times, even grabbed dinner once. He told me he lived in Barrie, but stayed in Toronto on the weekdays while he worked. We exchanged cell numbers and spoke occasionally. I only knew him for about two months. He never liked having his picture taken. His reason, he said was because he didn't think he looked good. In fact, he was very jumpy if anyone tried to take a picture. It seemed pretty odd, but I was busy with life and work and never really gave it a lot of thought beyond that fact that it was odd.

One weekend, my girlfriend invited me to her cottage for the weekend with some friends. I asked him if he would like to go. He said yes and we went and hung out for a few days, but he was always busy on his phone and, again, this behavior struck me as odd. The weekend came and went and even though things were pretty casual and cool with us, I had a nagging feeling inside something wasn't right. Monday arrived and I did something brave and bold, I went to the construction site where he worked and I asked someone very nonchalantly where he was. I knew he was way up high and not on the main level of this building. The guy asked me if I needed to speak with him, I said no, but I asked him point blank if he was married and the guy hesitated for a second and then said yes.

It was a shot in the dark, a question I hadn't even considered before I arrived on site. Then like a lightning bolt, the thought was there and the words were slipping from my lips. Now, everything made sense. I looked him up in the Yellow Pages online in Barrie and there he was, in plain day, his number and address. Completely in awe of his deceit, I texted him his own address and phone number. He quickly messaged me back. He tried to explain that he had been so captivated by me that he didn't have time in his head to tell me he was married.

You don't ask women out for coffee or flirt with someone with intention if you are married. Later, it occurred to me that I should have asked if he was married. The problem is, one would assume when someone doesn't wear a wedding ring, there's no tan line on their ring finger and they ask you out, that they're single. After I gave him a good verbal lashing, I told him to never speak to me again, or ever show his face near my work place again. I warned him if he ever tried to make his presence known to me, then I would make my presence known to his wife. Part of me wondered why I didn't call her, but truthfully, I didn't want the drama in my life. Every woman deserves to know when her guy is cheating, but what if she didn't believe me? I never asked for problems and I wasn't about to create more for myself. I just wanted to move on...and I did.

Baller Jerk

On my way home after work one day, I stopped for gas. Slightly tired and in no rush, I was slow to get out of the car and pump the gas. I leaned on the car and looked around at everyone else tending to their vehicles. At first, I saw no one of real interest to me. When I glanced over to the cars closest to me, I noticed a guy staring at me through his shades while he pumped gas into his BMW. I stared back through my own glasses, because I never shy away from a good stare down. This guy was cute and it caught me off guard a bit. I was pumping gas, after a long day, feeling shabby....and someone was staring at me despite my raggedness. I was intrigued.

As a bold woman, when a man is brave enough to stare at me, it always takes me back initially. I keep my guard up, but I'll be the first to admit, it does make my head turn. He smiled at me and we both finished up. He paid at the pump and I needed to go in. I could see him while I was still inside paying. The game of cat and mouse continued. After I paid, I approached my car. He got out and invited me to go for a coffee with him. Because I was tired, I declined, but we exchanged names and numbers. I didn't see any harm in having a coffee at some point.

Baller and I dated for a few months; he didn't even make it to the six-month deadline that I used to give most men. During the time we dated, he came across as somewhat shady. He didn't have his own place. I overlooked it. He lived with an ex-girlfriend out of convenience. I don't judge, so we never went there. Although I met her a few times and she was nice, it still seemed odd to me. There were lots of little things about him I initially overlooked. Mostly because deep down, I began my tally.

The tally is my mental board I use when things don't add up. Even though I don't focus on them and carry on, it doesn't mean I'm completely oblivious to it. It just means I gave you a chance and it's up to you to win me over. Just because I go out with or date someone has never meant that I'm convinced of their sincerity or devotion. It means they piqued my interest and I was curious enough to investigate who they are as a person. I never go into the relationship with the belief that it's forever. That's never been my experience.

In my mind, there's always doubt. With the baller I was never optimistic about how honest he was. My curiosity to see what he was all about got the best of me. I was in a relationship that lasted under six months and I never put much thought into any future with him so when things came to an abrupt ending, I wasn't surprised. Nor was I surprised with how it ended. The baller liked to play basketball and often hung out with his buddies.

We planned to hang out after he played ball. I had some random question to ask him, so I called him on the phone. After a brief conversation we hung up, or so he thought. Actually, I paused when I noticed that he hadn't hung up yet. Unsure if he had something else to say, I waited on the phone and heard something going on. I listened and what I heard was unsettling. Baller must have placed his phone in his hoodie, because I could hear him clear as day. Everyone was talking loud and hyped up after their game. It was easy to identify his voice.

Truth be told, they were all bragging about this and that. He recently replaced his BMW with an Audi and the guys told him he shouldn't have done that, that he should've kept the BMW. He bragged about how he got so much more action with the Audi than with the BMW. By action, I won't justify his classification of what kind, other than referencing felines. Yeah, the P-word. Offensive, isn't it? I couldn't believe my ears, because, he traded the BMW in for the Audi when he was already with me. Something triggered inside me and I hung up the phone. I called his friend and asked him to have Baller call me. Baller called me back with his cooler than cool tone. I recounted what happened and he explained to me that that was just shop talk.

Truly, that could be what it was, but who in their right mind wants a man who speaks like that about women? Offended was the very least of what I was feeling at that moment. How vulgar and rude, how disrespectful to me in front of his friends. If I were to forgive that, I'd be letting myself down and setting precedence that it's okay to talk like that about women. It's not, in fact, it's vile to even speak words like that into the universe about women. Whether someone hears it or not, it echoes a negative vibration and women will eventually feel it.

He apologized and begged me to forgive him for what he said, he even cried tears. Crocodile tears, as far as I was concerned. Regardless of how upset he was, and I believe he was to a degree; it was too little too late. Next came the gratuitous offer to buy me dinner so he could try and make it up to me. Not convinced of his sincerity in the least, I allowed him to take me to an expensive restaurant and heard him out. He talked, a lot. I listened to everything he had to say. Strong in my conviction, when he dropped me off at my door that night, I got out, looked at him and reaffirmed I was finished with the relationship.

I hope the Baller changed his ways and gained some knowledge to apply for the next girl.

Beachy Jerk

Another brief lesson learned is that some men will say and do whatever they can to get you into bed with them. I was with a few girls one day at the beach when we met a bunch of pretty cute guys. One particular guy seemed pretty smitten with me and there were equal guys to girls this time and everyone's interest seemed to be in different people which worked out well. This guy was visiting from another city and was staying at a house that he and some friends rented. We hit it off right away and there was a synergy between us, the kind that summer romances are made of.

Lucky in Love

We met at the beach and ended up chatting each other up with everyone else. It was a great day filled with sun, volleyball and a few drinks too. We all decided to go back to their rental house and hang out for the rest of the afternoon. They were all a few years older than us. They immediately had more game than us and by that, I mean more than volleyball. The afternoon of music turned into an evening of hanging out and many of us all crashed there, unable to drive. He assured me he would drive me back the next day and I thought, *cool, why not?* We ended up spending an entire long weekend together. I went home, only to be picked up by him again within a few hours. His crew were a lot of fun. My friends and I went back to their place another night and hung out together. He and I spent our remaining nights together at the beach.

Our parting was kind of bittersweet with lots of emotion. He was charming, kind and said some pretty amazing things to me over the course of the weekend that I believed. It was surprising to me when he got home that I didn't hear from him for a couple of days. Eventually, he called. We only spoke a few times on the phone after he left and both times were brief. He eventually dropped the bomb that he decided to get back with his ex. Talk about a crushing blow. Here I was, still a young girl who got swept off her feet. He had lyrics for days and swooned me hour after hour and even planned to come visit.

This guy literally made my head spin around with all the lyrics he dished me. Needless to say, I never spoke to him again, but his was one name I remembered. My lesson learned this time was often summer romances that start at the beach can end up leaving you with sand in your hair and dirt in your face. I said I never forgot his name right? Of course not. Certain jerks you remember, even if you don't want to.

Fast forward to later in life, I was in Toronto, working a special event at a car show with a bunch of girls all dolled up and being hostesses to the crowds. Out of nowhere, Mr. Beach appeared. I was shocked to see him on the floor so close to me. We made eye contact. He hovered around a bit before he made his way over to my area. I composed myself, drew my thoughts together and knew immediately what I was going to do.

I turned to face him and there he stood in front of me, still just as cute as ever and that beaming grin that swept me off my feet years ago, that and his pretty cool hair. I turned to him as we exchanged smiles and said hello. I returned his pleasantries and stuck out my hand, "Hello and you are?" The look on his face was priceless. I acted like I never met him before in my life, shook his hand and then said some stuff about the exhibit area we were in. I was polite, calm and cool and I did that, because I didn't know him. The person he presented himself to be was not who he really was, a conclusion I reached after pulling myself together from the heartbreak. I went on about my work and never turned back to look at him or what he was doing. That was the end of the Beachy Jerk.

The End of the Jerks

For any young teenage girls reading this, or someone who had a horrible teen life during the high school years, please take comfort in knowing you're not alone. I had some good friends in high school, but not a lot of them. I took comfort in knowing that the close friends I did have really cared about me. I found high school much like a prison to me. I was living and trying to be involved with everyone inside, but I was only living and not really alive.

Being a teenager is hard for anyone. This lifetime of damage made it ten times harder, in my opinion. I had no self-awareness, no self-esteem, no self-worth and I was completely numb inside. I had ten years of mental, physical, and sexual abuse clouding my thoughts and impairing my judgment. Any teenage boy that offered me the time of day in those days made me feel like I was something. Otherwise, I felt like I was nothing. That's what I was told throughout my life. The torturous words engrained in my brain that I was no good, not good enough, or good for nothing. Yet, despite this hideous programming, somehow I excelled in my public school years. I managed to keep my sanity as I focused on academics and sports. At school, I controlled my destiny and it balanced how I felt at home, which was empty and horrible.

Chapter 3: GETTING OUT OF DODGE

After bouncing from one jerk to another and then just plain spinning out of control and drowning in my own misery, I had to get out of my hometown. The extreme emotions I had to navigate through during my teens made it challenging to have a relationship with anyone. I worked hard weekly to heal from the pain. But, my pain proved to be a beacon for unhealthy and unhappy people. When you're not happy or in love with yourself, you can't love anyone else. I never knew that growing up, and I felt if I kept trying, eventually I would get it right.

What I should have done was take off to live as a Buddhist and just purge all the pain from my body and soul. Being sexually, physically and mentally abused throughout my formidable years had a major impact on how I felt about myself. Inside, I was tough as steel, I know that now. That's what gave me the strength to endure all those years of abuse without killing myself.

Of course, given my life experience and the emotional aftermath, I attracted some unhealthy people. I'm sure I appeared weak and vulnerable to some, yet inside I was anything but. This is how the conflict would come about in the first place between me and the "bad ones." The "bad ones" thought I was weak and vulnerable and tried to control me by being nice. Their agenda always had a price tag attached to their kindness. The price was for me to be at their beck and call and do as they say. That was never going to happen, even if a request was logical, because I was in my rebel mode.

The dire need to rebel from the type of authority and dictatorship I had lived under my entire life seeped into my soul and leaked into every relationship I ever found. I'd never been allowed to go to friend's houses, birthday parties and I never had a birthday party ever growing up. Relatives rarely came to visit me as they were not welcomed either. The villain liked to keep me prisoner under his control. Even when my mother went into the city from the farmhouse, I wasn't allowed to go with her. Too much time away from the villain again would weaken his hold over me, or so he thought. Yet, for ten years, I stayed and took it daily, weekly, monthly, and yearly. It was grueling most days.

So, I lived with this, and eventually attracted a guy who was not nice at all. In my quest to tell my story, it crossed my mind to not write about this person. I didn't want to give him any acknowledgement, he didn't deserve any. But to share my lessons, I realize I have to tell the stories. He was not the best looking guy by any means, and he wasn't the smartest by any stretch of the imagination. In retrospect, there was nothing special at all about him except the lesson I learned. Being with him taught me to watch my back and don't let my guard down.

If you think there is a potential someone will become hostile with you physically, you need to know their boundaries and what safety issues that could arise. If it's this bad, you need to put protections in place. In some situations, it may mean going to the police. When I finally split with this guy, it was after he had gotten physical with me on one occasion. I made a promise to myself that no one would ever touch me again the way the villain had and get away with it. Many people who have endured abuse struggle with advocating for their own safety. Even with years of therapy, there is a part of you that wants to avoid the conflict and run far away from the constant threat. The rage festering inside me made it easy to stick to my resolution that I would never tolerate it again, most of the time. This one situation caught me off guard.

When we split up; he stalked me. He had others stalk me. He wrote obscene things on my apartment door, stole my mail, and had other people make threats that they would cause harm to me. He was relentless. In hindsight, when he put his hands on me I should have called the police and charged him and been done with it. Unfortunately, I didn't and eventually it got so bad, that he even had his new girlfriend's friends harassing me. There was a change in the tide though when they eventually split up and she and her friends wanted to throw him under the bus too.

The police got involved and worked a plan to gather evidence to have him charged. In fact, a couple of them were ready to testify in court against him and at that moment, all I wanted to do was leave town. It wasn't worth going to court and I just wanted to be rid of this guy forever. I had some great opportunities come my way and so I left my hometown.

My grandmother's best friend, Murina, lived in a neighboring town and it was just far enough away to get me away from all of the drama and so I left. When I was twenty-years old, for the sake of my sanity, I literally disappeared out of my hometown to go and discover who I was. Murina also had introduced me to a guy my age who worked with her and we began dating. I considered it added encouragement to leave my hometown. We dated for a while but the romance fizzled out.

Murina had a daughter who I had grown up knowing and she was like a cousin to me. I worked for her at her tanning salon as well as at a fitness center. I had a small bachelor pad and lived very modestly as I trudged along and settled into an even smaller town than the one I had grown up in. It was very close to the big city, so it felt like I was a step closer to freedom. I only lived in that small town long enough to go to college, had a few failed romances and would finally meet my first big love, Karlof. Then I ran to the big city and stayed there for almost eighteen years.

During the time I lived in that small town, I shed my skin, grew as a person, and managed to peel back the layers of damage and protective shields to reveal who I truly was along the way. Most of this self-discovery involved trudging through a heavily dense forest with tons of bush. I stumbled, tripped, staggered, fell, was scraped up, and bruised by the time I finally found a clearing.

It was all worth it. I learned my personal value and I finally acknowledged just how resilient I was. If my childhood didn't do me in, then no relationship would either. As time went on, I grew more defiant to love and I didn't bat an eye when a relationship ended. It became evident to me at the start of every relationship, there was going to be an end. It was just a matter of time before it would happen. Deep down inside, I had zero confidence in men. I was always on alert for signs of when the end was near. Not a great way to live your life, but it was what I came to expect from people.

We'll talk about Karlof in the chapter, *For the Love of an Accent*. He was the one who I graded everyone else against in the years that would follow and one of my biggest regrets. In fact I can't pass through that town without thinking of him and for a long time Karlof would slip into my thoughts when I least expected it.

Chapter 4: KEEPING TIME TO THE BEAT OF THE MUSIC

I love the sound of a good drum. There is something about the richness of the melodic tones of the skin of the drum and the seductiveness of the symbol and the high hat has made my heart beat faster and skin tingle. It's a unique instrument and men who can play it are also unique in their own way as well. For starters, it has been said that rock steady drummers can actually be smarter than other musicians. Over the years, I had read about researchers who had drummers play a variety of different beats and then tasked them with a simple sixty-problem intelligence test. The drummers who scored the highest were also better able to keep a steady beat.

When I fell for a drummer, it wasn't just because he was a good musician. The ones I liked were quite smart. It's no wonder then that I fell for not one, but three drummers. They were very different men. One, a more traditional drummer, we will call him Junior and the other two were all about Rock n Roll. According to a few different articles I came across over the years, a steady drummer may be more intelligent than their other band mates, the drummer's gifts can be shared: a tight beat can actually transfer that natural intelligence to others. So maybe, each was like an educational program of sorts.

Junior

While living in Toronto, I met Junior. I was in my late twenties and floating around the city, single with no plans or interest in meeting anyone. I'd been casually dating men with no real second dates and I wasn't taking anyone too seriously. I was focused on my career and involved in my pursuit of being an established journalist. After a few casualties in the love department, I didn't want any more for a while. In my pursuit of journalism, I was invited to many events and I was covering Fashion Week one year, which is a hustle and bustle of action. Fabulous clothes, music and most of all beautiful women. It was also the feeding ground for Junior because he loved all three so passionately. He used fashion and music to attain the beautiful women. He had many before me and continued to have many more beautiful women after me.

I always believed he'd die a lonely man when he got old, ugly and ran out of women. Deep inside, I found it troubling. I thought one man shouldn't be allowed to use up all the beautiful women only for his own selfish ego stroking monster and ruin them for everyone else.

From my seat in the front row, I watched the show and took in the beauty of the surroundings. I was swooned by the steady beat of drums accompanying the models. My gaze collided with one handsome, dreadlocked drummer. The depth of his stare from his intense, brown eyes would make most women look away from his gaze.

Not me. I met his gaze with my own powerful and self-assured stare. He told me later how that intrigued him. I'm sure some women would have blushed from the bold contact. Not me. I let him know I saw him looking at me and there was heat between us. The show ended and he made his way over to me. Compliments ensued. Junior told me he liked how I looked, he loved my hair…he wanted me, but settled for my number. He probably collected others' numbers too, but mine was his quest at the moment. I relinquished my seven digits to him as I was intrigued by his voice and his eccentric charisma. Junior had a sensual charm that oozed from his soft voice and the way in which he spoke to me. Unlike some of the others, over the course of our romance, he never raised his voice to me.

Junior was fun. He played in lots of dance clubs and I loved to dance. He loved when I danced during his performances, and I found that titillating. Kind of a foreplay that occurred often and it was fun. But, I wasn't the only one he watched. He liked to watch all the beautiful women dance. He often spoke of others to me, and was intent on having a threesome at some point. This is how he communicated his idea of an "open relationship." He wanted me and the option of sleeping with others and saw nothing wrong with it. I never agreed to any of it at any time, but he of course, thought he would eventually sway me to his darker side.

At least the women he pointed out to me were attractive. He often asked, "What about her? Do you like this one? What about your girlfriend so and so?" As time moved on, he wore me down. Not to participate. It got to the point of not liking him anymore. I found his quest to fill his emptiness troubling. We carried on a relationship for about six months, which was my typical cut-off time for relationships.

Our break finally came one day at the video store. I was at the front checking out a movie, he was roaming around still looking for a second movie, or so he led me to believe. Instead, he was on the phone, talking to someone. This time, his gaze towards me was so different than the first time we met. It looked pensive and deceitful. I could tell. I gestured to him to come to the counter and he was slow to move. Junior eventually made his way to the counter, but my Spidey-sense was tingling, so-to-speak. As we drove back to watch movies for the afternoon, I wondered. At the time, we lived together, albeit briefly, more of a situation of circumstances than actually wanting on my part.

We spent the afternoon watching movies. He had to work that night and usually left late. I had a morning job that required me to go to bed quite early. He left for his gig. As I started to drift off to sleep, that cold feeling of betrayal crept into my head. I got up, went to the drawer where he kept condoms and counted them.

Always trust your inner voice. I went to work, and came home early. The following evening came and it was time for him to play another venue. His friend was running late, so he borrowed my car. Once he left, I went to the drawer, I counted again and there were two missing. I couldn't believe it. I counted a second time and then I picked up the phone and called him. He answered and I asked him if he has made it to the gig yet?

"No, almost there," he said.

"Oh good, do you have everything?"

"Yes, he replied, why do you ask?"

"You have everything, you're sure?" There was no confusion in my tone, I'm sure it held more anger than anything else at that point. My blood was boiling.

His voice changed, and I knew he got what I was saying "What?" he barked.

"You have your condoms for your night out?"

His reply was charming. "Fuck you, Orlena."

What a play on words, I thought. *On the contrary my soon-to-be former lover. You won't ever be doing that again with me.* I told him to turn my car around and bring it back.

"I don't care at this point if you're late for you gig or whatever, I'm done. Bring my car back; take a cab to your gig."

When he finally dropped the car off he tried to argue I knew all along that he was into an open relationship. He insisted I couldn't be mad at him for what he naturally wanted to do and he never hid those desires from me. We both knew I never agreed to his terms. I never wanted to participate and I never wanted to share him with anyone.

No girlfriend wants to feel like the anchor and accessory in their man's life, while he searches for his next conquest. It would have been different perhaps if I fancied another man and let him know. Nonetheless, his constant ogling of other women stole the sparkle of our relationship. It lost its luster quickly. Once again, I was attracted to someone who was all wrong for me. I wanted to be the person I thought he was looking for. I thought I was it. In the end, I wasn't. Junior was one of those guys who will always be looking, lusting and wanting what he can't have. From what I hear from people who know him and what I see on social media, he is in my opinion, pretty much the same.

I was one of the women he thought he couldn't have, until he had me and then he wanted someone else. I'm not sure if someone like that ever settles down, or will ever be happy with himself or who he's with. I feel like each person he is with is a trophy of sorts and once it loses its shine to him, he wants a new one. I'm thankful it's not my problem anymore.

Rock n' Roll

Rock n' Roll is sexy and irresistible to many. I have dated two different guys who were Rock n Roll drummers. One was very successful, the other not so much, (which is also why I won't really talk about the other). It was so short-lived and uninteresting to me, that it would be boring to read. The third was the tryst. It would never have lasted anyway, as he was always on tour with some band or another and always touring the world. However, one Rock n Roller had a soul, kept his emotions in check, and was a warm, kind person. He struck me as a drifter who would never settle down in a traditional sense. Instead he would just enjoy a life of music, discovering the world and living the life of a musician.

I couldn't picture him owning his own house, marrying or having children. Let's call him R&R. I first met him while I was with a friend of his. We never shared longing looks or anything like that while I was attached. There was, however, always something I found enticing about him. Perhaps he was the forbidden fruit that you dare not touch. Nonetheless, we got together after the breakup, but much later.

R&R and I finally got together, by a few invitations to some of the places where he would be performing. A few times, we chatted and got to know each other a little better. It was a dance of attraction, that's for sure. Forbidden, lovers because he was friends with one of my exes who happened to be quite hostile. The ex was in jail at that time and could do no harm to either of us while we flirted with the idea of being together. I kept things friendly, while I secretly lusted for him. I could see in his eyes on several occasions that he was wearing down with his struggle to resist me.

Lucky in Love

One night he offered for me to come over and have dinner together and I knew that it was on. I thought dinner would not be a long drawn out one, but I was wrong. I arrived and he was still cooking some fabulous, organic and healthy food for us to fuel up on. He was calm, cool and collected while I sat at the table and watched him move about. Our dinner lasted a couple of hours, while we ate, talked, sipped wine and teased each other with flirtatious stares. R&R had such a soft, sensual aroma to him. The kind you get from natural soaps, lotions and oils, which he used faithfully. His skin was smooth and supple, and he had the most exotic look to him.

Dessert never came, but his lips met mine with such sweetness, I didn't need to taste sugar. His caress was strong, yet tender. I could feel all the resistance of the years slip away into nothing more than a hazard of thoughts. His body was lean, sculpted and perfect. Like a chiseled statue and every curve of him was delicious to look at. Our love affair was fueled by passion, by intensity and by the concept that maybe it wasn't meant to be. Sometimes the sweetest fruit is the most forbidden as we would soon find out, it can have a bitter aftertaste.

Our many dinners in and evenings filled with music at local venues were interlaced with passionate romance. I felt my heart warming to the idea of this guy in my life, but how could that happen? With someone we both knew to be leaving jail soon, it was only a matter of time before this would have to end. R&R did on one occasion visit him to tell him that we had been seeing each other. I was surprised at his confession, but I suppose the guilt was too much for him. We were two people who liked each other, enjoyed dinners and romance, but deep down, I knew there was something missing. It would never have worked. There was too much drama attached to the prospect of being together.

Eventually, life got in the way, along with my gut feeling that he would never allow himself to be close to me or love me. We would be friends later and still remain friends.

South Paw

My South Paw (SP) drummer was not only left handed, he was also from the Deep South. Atlanta, to be exact. He was a fun guy I met online during a time I was single, and when online dating was relatively new. I had heard about it from others and thought *why not?* Curious about how well it would pan out, I put up a profile and checked it all out. I was twenty-nine years old and thirty loomed in front of me like a fog that I was scared to go into. A blanket of dread shrouded me as I wondered what lay ahead and would I be alone. Turning thirty for me was a scary time. Like so many women conditioned to associate age with life milestones, I thought not being married and turning thirty was the marker for being a spinster forever. In my bid to avoid this fate, I set about searching online for someone who was interesting enough that I wouldn't get bored of them. It's not surprising that I fell for a drummer; in fact, he was the first one I fell for and the others came later.

South Paw was a light-skinned, southern rocker guy who was tall, lean and had short blonde hair. Complete with piercings and tattoos, he was raised in Atlanta, and played in a rock band. He was a constant contradiction in his demeanor. I say this because the way he looked and the lifestyle he lived, he seriously didn't know how good looking he was. A rare factor for a rocker in those days.

It was doomed from the start, as he had zero self-esteem. I learned this through many subtle ways on the surface. He was deeply insecure. I visited him a few times and on the second last occasion I saw him, he asked me a question I was not prepared for, I never saw it coming. I had put it out into the universe that I didn't want to turn thirty alone, and here was South Paw making sure that didn't happen. Careful what you wish for in life, because chances are, you will get it.

It was a hot summer's day in the south and we had gone to church with his family. Southern Gospel church is an experience in and of itself. A good old' gospel church experience that comes complete with the most exuberant singing, floor shaking, and joyous emotions that you can possible imagine will happen when true Southern folk go to church. They put it all out there. I visited him in Atlanta on two different occasions. Once I flew down for a short period of time, and on the second and final time throughout the four months we dated, I drove down to stay for a week. I got to see his life, his work, his family and met his child that lived with the mother. I got a good feel for who South Paw was on the inside.

What didn't resonate that well with me was the person he's already had a child with. He was young when he became a father. The woman he chose to sleep with was probably one of the least desirable women on this planet. I imagined having to spend my life being connected to this woman. It was not the pretty fairytale I had envisioned or searched for.

Let's fast forward this story to a day in the middle of the visit. We were at a barbecue with all of his family and some of his friends. South Paw's mom was like Blanche from the Golden Girls; soft and super feminine with quick wit and a killer smile. Everyone was there and it was going to be quite a barbecue with all the true southern fixings, including grits. The sun was shining and we were taking in the beauty of the day and enjoying food, when the music stopped.

When I looked around, I saw South Paw standing there and then everything seemed to happen in slow motion.

A series of questions fired off in my head like, what was in his hand? What was he doing? Why is he bending down? Why is everyone staring at me and I began to feel sick to my stomach, and not because of all the southern fried chicken. South Paw was on bended knee, asking me to marry him in front of all his relatives. Good God! He looked so happy and so self-assured. Did I mention everyone was looking at me with huge smiles on their faces?

The next thing I know, I guess I said yes, although I don't remember doing it. I think I just smiled back at him and he hugged me. Then everyone applauded. Okay, at this point, I'm engaged with his grandmother's wedding ring on my finger. The next few days I was there visiting with South Paw and his family, I thought to myself, I did ask for this by not wanting to turn thirty and be single. I can remember the distinct feeling this had to be a dream as I drove back to Toronto.

Thank God, I decided to drive down this time, because I needed the drive home to comprehend what the hell just happened and how I was going to get out of this. There were many reasons I didn't want to marry this guy. He didn't seem to have any direction, he was poorly paid at his job, and he had a child with a kind of backwoods woman. No. No, no. Swift and immediate was all I could think of. I arrived back in Toronto and the very next day, called his mother and told her I simply couldn't do this and asked her if she even thought that this was a good pairing.

Relief washed over me when she answered "no." She would love to have me as a daughter in law, but she admitted that her son was not ready to marry anyone and certainly not me. I mailed the ring back with a letter for him. South Paw was never to be seen again......and The Beat Goes on.......

A Legend's Son

The beat goes on still, just in a different medium–singing. I grew up loving music, listening to it, singing in the choir at school and playing the accordion with the Ontario Conservatory of Music for almost eight years. I always had an appreciation for anyone with musical talent, because I understood the dedication it took to become really good. In becoming really good at something, there can sometimes also come ego. A particular Canadian singer-songwriter legend had a son who had an ego bigger than his father's talent.

If this particular man's dad knew the way in which he spoke to women, I think he would have to rewrite a few songs of his and quite possibly make his son sing them over and over again to drill into his head how women should be spoken to. This particular artist had some minor fame in a band in Canada before he would venture back to Europe after his songs lost their luster. I had my online news magazine at the time, which would be called a blog now, and I was interviewing all kinds of interesting artists.

When the opportunity came up to interview this guy and his band, I jumped at it, having no idea what he was like without a microphone. I interviewed the band earlier in the day and they invited me and a few others to their mini-concert later that night. I brought my close girlfriend with me and we ventured out into the night.

The band had some pretty popular songs at the time and my girlfriend and I enjoyed the music that night. We decided to hang out a bit after at the encouragement of the guys. We hung out and enjoyed some drinks, talked about music, cities and idle chit-chat. It was lots of fun until the conversation shifted between the "legend's son" and myself. The mood went from fun to naughty all in a few short whispers. I am not saying he wasn't attractive and alluring, it's just he went from zero-to-a hundred in a few sentences. He told me he found me sexy and wasn't into having sex with anyone at this time in his life.

Stunned, I thought to myself, *where did this come from all of a sudden? Thanks for the confirmation that you're not having sex with anyone, I wasn't asking.* I laughed uncomfortably and brushed it off, but he went on. He whispered to me that he would love to grind his body all over mine and said it in a derogatory kind of way.

It was unpleasant at best, and I wasn't interested in being someone's pleasure cushion for their own enjoyment. I was in shock and disappointed that he didn't exhibit the same level of class his father had, sadly. I guess he felt he could say whatever he wanted to whoever he wanted. I excused myself for the night left and never spoke to him again. His lead guitarist messaged me to ask why I had left so abruptly at the urging of the legend's son. I told him why and he laughed and then proceeded to hit on me too, in a more subtle way than his buddy. I thought, *what the heck is going on here? One and now the other.* I just shook my head and politely declined the offer.

I had gotten used to men responding to me in a sexual way, so his advances and behavior didn't really shock or bother me as much as it would for some. I was conditioned at a young age that I was a sexual being. I felt somewhat cursed in a sense, because men responded to me the same way most of the time. I naturally expected sex to be their agenda when they approached me, and I was always prepared for it.

When I initially moved to Toronto and started dating, that agenda seemed to remain. In fact, it got even stronger in my life. In an attempt to counteract this dynamic, I suppose at times, I intentionally drew men in, and then shot them down as self-defense, as my own way of gaining control back.

Maybe on a deeper level, I was perpetuating previous ideas that had been taught to me and in fact, weren't accurate. The villain had messed up most of how I responded to men. Many times, I thought I should give up on men and start dating women. I trudged on with men though, turning into a perpetual dater.

R&B, Hip Hop and Soul

Working as an entertainment journalist in a metropolitan city offers you an abundance of parties and invites to many social gatherings, both professional and personal. Once you have your credentials and keep a good rapport with entertainers, you have an invite to just about everything you want. In the course of all the events, parties and social gatherings, you do meet men that are lovely and sweet and you meet men that are dirty and edgy. Both are interesting to me. The dirty and edgy ones always challenge my intelligence, while the sweet and lovely ones are impressed by it. Both come across as intrigued with me, but for varying reasons.

There are two different sides to me when it comes to dealing with men, and the side each one gets depends on what type of guy they are. There's a dark side to me that resides within from my abusive and torturous childhood. That inner darkness is tempted by men who try and bring that out in me. That part of me wants power and control over whatever is trying to overtake my freedom and security. It's like a beast within me that gets awakened by power and I rise to match that power and overtake it with my personality. But, it is only temporary and it's not the overall makeup of who I am. It's like a switch that gets turned on and I don't want it on too long because it's exhausting and taps into something I would like to put to rest in me. Every time the villain would have his way with me, a piece of me would hide away from him and the fire would build around that piece and protect my sanity.

In the R&B, hip-hop, and soul world, there are two very distinct types of men: the "bad boys" and the "sweet boys," and the type of man I would meet was dictated and dependent on where I was in my life at that time, and how I was feeling that week or day.

Blend of 3

I remember meeting B3 when I was in my early thirties. A well-connected musician in the industry. He had some major success on radio with songs that are still played today. He was a blend of R&B, hip-hop, and soul. He was a sweet guy with a bad boy edge. That's why I conversed mostly with him by phone and the odd time in person. He was quite naughty on the phone and loved to spin his lyrical abilities to make me blush. I never did, but faked it for his amusement, and mine.

We were out one night and coming back from an event. We decided to take a stroll through a park nearby. It was an innocent walk for the most part. Like most parks, there were picnic tables and we sat down on a warm summer night and just kicked back and chatted. He was in one of his flirtatious moods and began speaking to me in such a way that it awakened that beast in me. I didn't feel uncomfortable or feel I was in any danger. In fact, I felt the opposite, powerful and alive.

I matched his wit and challenged his thoughts. He wanted to dance with words and tried to seduce me, so I turned it around on him. His response made me think he was thrilled with the challenge, but I lost interest in him. He was captivated by my words and soon by my lips and arms. I took control of what was going on. There was some ruffling of clothes and tempting suggestions from him. Common sense prevailed, and with one quick breath, I told him I had to be up early and needed to leave.

For me, the dance of words, passionate embrace and succumbing to my power and passion satiated my interest in him. I knew I was moving on from the idea of him in any other way than just a friendship. Like a typical man, rejected, he was intrigued and wanted to see me again and called me a few more times to pursue that idea. I dodged the pursuit until he grew tired and moved on.

Soul for Days

Soul for Days was a rebirth of a brother from the 1940's and 1950's and his music reflected just that, with a twist. My minor interactions with him were mostly at events and the odd time at a club if a live band was playing. What was most interesting about this man is how everything changed between the two of us over the course of a few hours one night. We were at a pretty big event and even though he was from the big city, he was living in the States at that time and staying at a hotel for the weekend. I had been there covering the entertainment news and was taking some down time in the lounge, when Soul for Days saddled up next to me and started asking me questions.

His words to me, and his body language seemed conflicted. He asked curious questions, however, seemed eager for quick answers. His eyes were an intense deep brown and had the most penetrating gaze, like he was looking deep inside me, or maybe right through me. I have met many men who have tried this technique on me and my darker side stirred within whenever someone wanted to dance with it. Since then, I've kept that darkness in a box and used it only when I am with someone I really love; otherwise, it can be dangerous to toy with.

On this night, he tempted me with his lust and desire. I wasn't entirely sure I wanted to play, but my interest was piqued. He asked if I wanted to take a walk with him and chat further. He had plans to go out to a party that was happening and wanted to know if I would walk back with him to his hotel room so he could get changed. I thought, *I'll play and see what he is up to.* I thought about going to the party, too, but it had been a long day already.

We walked, and talked and he tried to seduce me with his smooth moves and slick talk. He was oh-so-good with the lyrics in his songs and sincerely unforgettable. By the time we ended up at his hotel room, I wanted a drink. It had been a long day and I wanted to chill out and to keep my hands busy while he took a moment to get ready. Soul's room was a two-room split and big. There was a separate seating area from his room and bathroom area. One interesting feature of his room was that his shower had an all glass wall and that glass wall divided his bedroom area. I found this out when I first came into the room and thought that was pretty interesting.

Of course, he said he needed a quick shower. I proceeded to go into the sitting area when he insisted, I took a seat on the bed, enjoyed my drink and the show. *What show?* Turned out the show was of him showering in plain view so I could watch. I felt the devil that night tip-toeing on my shoulder and thought, *why not?* I saw and sipped. He dipped, slipped, and soaped himself for a few minutes, although it felt much longer. When he wrapped a crisp white towel around him and came around the corner, he walked right up to me, took the glass from my hands and put it on the dresser stand. I went to stand up and he grabbed me and pulled me close to his steamy, soft skin.

Those deep brown eyes stared so intensely into mine that I started to lose my grip on what was happening. He captured my lips with his, and the softness of them enveloped mine. The words to his songs danced in my head and I grew a little disoriented with the whole vibe of what was going on. His kiss grew more passionate and I could feel the intensity of something else at that moment too and pulled back.

"You should get ready and go to the party," I rasped. I was getting tired and I knew for a fact I was not going to sleep with this guy. Things had already skipped past where I thought they were going and his game was strong. He was adamant that he wanted to sleep with me, but neither of us were prepared for that and even if I was down, he would need to visit a store near-by.

My response was no. I was leaving and hoped he would still enjoy his night out and I had to be on my way. Soul was surprised by my sudden need to depart and I am sure not too many people had ever turned him down. In this case, the more someone wanted to sleep with me, the less I wanted to. I was flattered that he wanted to and departed knowing that. We spoke on the phone a few more times after that night. He had a few more hits on the radio and then he drifted out of the music scene much like he drifted out of my life.

Chapter 5: DANCING WITH THE LAW

Growing up in a house filled with volatile emotions, intense hostility and aggression made me dislike authority in the worst way. It was unpredictable all the time and nothing ever was the way it was supposed to be. There was no normal family life for me. Every day was different and the only thing that was certain was that I would be victimized in some way. Every day was the same in that regard.

My step-father was a pedophile that victimized me for ten years with such ferocity, that I never thought I was going to survive it. Many days and nights I prayed someone would rescue me from my life when I was younger. The villain loved to torture me. He would schedule beating times in the day for any little thing he felt I did wrong. Then I would be riddled with anxiety the whole day long waiting for the time to come that I would be beaten again. Often it would be after dinner. I would sit with the family eating dinner slowly and everyone at the table, the villain, his mother, who lived with us and my mother all knew another beating was in my near future, yet they all did nothing to protect me from it.

On those nights, I felt sick to my stomach sitting there waiting. I couldn't believe my own mother did nothing to stop it. She was afraid of him too. I ate and helped clean up dishes as the hands on the clock ticked down to my beating time. The villain's favorite way to beat me was with a belt. He had a piece of rubber from what appeared to be a belt off an engine of a vehicle. It was about two inches wide, red in color and about ten inches long. He even wrote in blue ink on it that it was to be used on me and named the three adults in the house that could use it to beat me with.

The beating sessions occurred in the garage and the walk from the house to my living hell was a short one. I was sure the neighbors heard me scream from the pain of the belt, yet no one came breaking down the door to stop it. Prior to the beating he would ask me why I was getting beat. He wanted me to recite to him why. I was so young when I started getting my beatings; as young as five years old. I would stand before him and he would have me put out my hands palms up. I confess, I can feel my anxiety building inside as I type this. I can remember the pain and I remember the fear. It's still a very real part of me.

He would whack the belt down on each of my hands several times, so hard and if I moved my hand even a little, or put my hands down to shake them from the pain, he would whip me even harder on that same hand again with the belt.

My mother stayed inside the house doing whatever she would be doing and the villain's mother was inside too. Neither of them did anything to stop him or save me. I was all alone in the garage with the villain at his mercy. He enjoyed beating me and the reason I know this is because of the sheer evil and anger-fueled pleasure portrayed on his face. He never consoled me after or hugged me at all. The villain carried a distinct self-entitlement for the beatings he gave me, and felt justified for each and every one of them and the extent of violence he dished out.

My life felt hopeless back then. I had endless beatings in that garage. Sometimes he would use the belt on my rear end. He would bend me over his lap and brace his leg over my two legs to hold me in place. Once the first lash would happen, I'd struggle to get away from his grip with all my might and would cry with such desperation. I can feel my tears and pain even to this day. I would love to be able to go back to those days, come from the future, run inside that garage, and save myself from him. Just kick down the door and grab that little girl and take her far away from him. I would love for him to feel that pain and see how he enjoyed it.

Sometimes he sexually abused me after he beat me too and forced me to please him. He sickened me in every way. I hated him more than anything or anyone. He even forced me to drink some strange liquid to wash his filth down. A liquid I later found out was cheap wine. It tasted disgusting. He was a disgusting man. He tried to break me with those beatings and abuse. He tried to crush my spirit and make me surrender. I may have had to obey him while I was in his miserable life, but he never broke my spirit. I was stronger than he was. I never gave up. I prayed to God every night after my beatings. I cried myself to sleep and wondered why I was living at all.

As I mentioned earlier, for years I didn't even have my own bedroom; a place I could hide and cry. I had to cry while in the presence of everyone. Being in a hallway also made me accessible to him when he wanted to sexually abuse me, which was almost daily. I don't remember very many days of my childhood where he didn't physically or sexually abuse me.

Some days, I look back and still can't believe I endured it all and can still laugh, smile, and love, even if it is only for a brief time. He instilled fear in me that men were not to be trusted and that love came from a place of lust, not from pure intimacy. I'm not even sure I truly understand the feeling of true intimacy.

Most people describe it as the most incredible feeling, a starburst of emotions inside, radiating from the outside in, and then a low burn. For me, I slowly feel all of those things while a fear builds inside me too. It's like a moth to a flame, burned by the fire. You want it, but you are afraid of it. In the rebuke of authority, there is also something familiar about it. Something familiar, but something you eventually dislike.

Add to it, the fact that the house I lived in with three adults who never protected me. I suppose the allure of having a man who could protect me in my life is naturally enticing. In lieu of that, being drawn to professions that offered protection wasn't a surprise for me.

Busted

Cops were always painted to us as children, as the protectors, heroes that will rescue you if only you call. I am not a *blues chaser* as many call women who like a man in uniform, but every now and then, like the craving for something sweet, I also crave the strength of one who likes to swoop in and save a damsel in distress. Who doesn't like a man in uniform?

On a few occasions, I was that damsel in distress. I can honestly say that the few who crossed my path were only a blip of interest and not worth mentioning at all. It's sad but so true. One boy in blue in particular, however, made me think twice about who is kicking down doors of drug busts. If only criminals knew the leisurely activities of some.

Let us call this deviant Bad Cop. He pursued me with intense flirtation at my workplace. We didn't work together per se, but we did cross paths on a few occasions. He was the traditional guys' guy. He had big dogs, big muscles, a big ego and a dark side. Who would have thought a man who liked fast cars, intense work and an adrenaline junkie of sorts, would be interested in what's in my closet and not his own.

The first few months we dated, he appeared with all the charm that he wanted me to believe about him. Bad Cop romanced me with dinners out, frequent text messages, emails and phone calls, all leading to a budding romance. Bad cop showered me with a constant flow of attention and little gifts here and there that he felt would win my affection and trust. It had been a few months when he surprised me with a request to dinner one evening.

During the day, he messaged me that he was at an adult novelty store and that he was picking up some special items for tonight and asked if I like leather. *Oooh, so he likes leather*, I thought. *What next whips and chains? Bondage? Whatever floats your boat,* I thought? We are adults here, so it doesn't matter to me. I arrived at his house later that day around six o'clock in the evening. I knocked with a slight hesitation, not knowing what was on the other side.

Nothing would prepare me for what I would see. The door opened and I will never forget the sight of him. He stood there with his muscles glistening and no shirt on. However, he also had on a pair of sheer nylons, a tight leather skirt and red heels. I thought for a moment, *maybe I should leave.* Curiosity got the best of me, I was interested to know what was going to happen next. He was not effeminate in his manner, but he asked if I liked what I saw.

"You look really good in those nylons," I offered. You have to compliment someone when they go to that much work to make a nice dinner and look good. He escorted me to the table with a saunter in his heels—a saunter many women aspire to master in heels, I might add!

It was a far cry from the swagger I was used to seeing him in when he had jeans, a t-shirt, and boots on. He busied himself at the stove in the kitchen, plated the food, and brought it to the table. I thought to myself, *where is this going to go now?* He crossed his legs at the table, ran his hands down his legs and asked me to feel his legs. The sensation of wearing nylons was one that made him feel really good, he confessed. I have to admit, his legs looked really good in the nylons too. I think he even made the effort to shave.

How he could sit at the table in the tight leather skirt I had no idea. I relaxed into the idea of dining with him, because this was going to be the last time I ever saw him. I can't be with a man who portrays himself as one way and without warning suddenly flips it like that. Give a girl some notice and let me know you are a cross-dresser. Give me the option to pass. Don't assume every girl is going to be into it. On the flip side, I wouldn't recommend you introduce it too early in a relationship either. I later found out that he was suffering from Post-Traumatic Stress Disorder. I can't help but wonder if perhaps this helped him relax.

Don't get me wrong, there is no shame in things that please people when it doesn't harm others. I realize it took a lot of courage for him to share this side of him. It was just a lot for me to handle. I admit, it caught me off guard as it wasn't something I expected from a big strong man who worked for the police.

I can't even explain the series of events that happened after dinner, but I can say, I was entertained by his behavior and requests. After that night, I ran away fast and never looked back.

Mr. Wonderful

Working in Toronto as a spokesperson and model for a number of years allowed me to meet a wide variety of people. Traveling to gigs wasn't always smooth sailing. On one occasion, I was in the middle of a campaign that would last all summer for Budweiser. There was always three Budweiser girls touring for the brand; "Bud, Wei, and Sir," for anyone who was familiar with the reference. Yes, I was a Budweiser Girl and was mostly Bud. I had to pick up a girl that day and the traffic was busy that morning. Unbelievably so, and no one seemed to be paying attention as to why. At a yellow light, as we went through the intersection someone smashed into the front of us.

They didn't cause a ton of damage, but nonetheless, a police officer, Mr. Wonderful arrived on the scene and the look on his face was priceless. There stood Bud and Wei, with our white crop tops and red short shorts and sneakers standing beside the car. It was funny enough, because we asked ourselves why this happened on our way to a gig at the head office, of all places.

Mr. Wonderful proved himself fantastic by the way he handled the situation and he looked every bit like what you would expect the perfect cop to look like. Tall, blue eyed, handsome and fit. He took down all the information and got things sorted out for us quickly because we were on a timeline. Delayed from the accident, we were now going to be late. Luckily there were no charges laid and the other driver agreed to pay for the damages to my vehicle.

My next question was how are we supposed to get to head office? There was no time to rent a car and get there on time. We batted our lashes at Mr. Wonderful and he was so nice that he offered to drive us to the brewery. We weren't that far from downtown and when you're travelling in a cruiser, you're going to arrive there that much faster. He was nice enough to put some paper towel in the back seat and told us not to touch anything because it was filthy back there. He said the back of the cruiser was one of the dirtiest places you could sit in. We had a ride so we weren't being picky at all.

We arrived to head office, photos were taken, the story was shared with our tour manager and the beer reps, and the amusement of the story superseded us being late. Mr. Wonderful had given us his business card to follow up with any questions he might have or vice-versa. I reached out the next day and left a message of gratitude before I headed to the gym.

At the time I lived at The Grange, which was right downtown off Queen Street and just a few steps from MuchMusic. It was right in the heartbeat of the city. I could easily walk to the gym in the morning from the place I was staying at and that's where I headed shortly after I hung up the phone. Down the elevator I went and out the front door and proceeded to cross the road. I noticed a cruiser to the right of the building, but thought nothing of it. I walked down the street at a good pace and noticed that the cruiser had pulled up behind me slowly. I stopped and glanced over to discover Mr. Wonderful behind the wheel.

He said he'd just got my message and since my address information had been taken down, he thought it would be ok to stop by my place. I was surprised and told him he didn't have to come by. I was a little nervous as I was only in my early twenties and he was in his forties. Not nervous in a scared sort of way, but nervous in a way an older man might make a younger woman feel. He asked if I would go for a coffee sometime. I said yes, so I could finish our awkward exchange and get to the gym. It was also my way to regain control of the conversation. Now I would have to call him if I wanted to go, which I was slightly nervous to do so. I said my goodbyes and went to the gym.

I felt strange because, he worked in the area and knew where I lived and there really wouldn't be much I could do to divert his attention. Eventually I agreed to go for coffee with Mr. Wonderful. I felt no harm in humoring him and I didn't know a lot of people in the city and figured knowing a cop wouldn't be a bad thing. Mr. Wonderful called me at my girlfriend's place at different times in between our coffee dates. The conversations were always pretty forward and he often eluded to wanting some kind of romance with me. I wasn't interested at all, but was always polite with him.

A few weeks had passed and I hadn't heard from him or seen him on my street, so. I assumed his interest had waned and he had dropped the idea. On one sunny day, I left my building, and out the front door, across the street was a cruiser...again. It was Mr. Wonderful. He pulled up and was all smiles, happy to see me. I jested maybe he found a new beer of choice? He proceeded to tell me that he had been away on holiday.

Good, I thought, as it gave me a break from phone calls. He then told me it wasn't just a holiday he had gone on vacation and had gotten married. *Excuse me? Married?* When over the course of coffees, conversation and trolling for me did he ever say he was with someone or was planning to marry someone? Never, is the answer. I instantly felt sad for whomever he married and hid my disgust with his behavior. I gave him my congratulations and instantly jogged away from him and out of sight....for good. He never called me again and I never saw him in my neighborhood again. Who knows if he watched me around the neighborhood after that day, I would have no idea, I was just glad I never saw him. So much for being Mr. Wonderful.

Judge, no Jury

Sexual predators don't just seek conquests out through dating. Although this experience wasn't romantically inclined, this person's agenda proved to be one in the same of the other men in my life. For that reason only, I felt the need to share this in my story. Not that it's a surprise to anyone, but there are some people in the criminal justice system with their own, hidden, sinister agendas. To have power, gives some people a sense of entitlement with their roles of authority.

While I lived in Toronto, I had accumulated some parking infractions. If you know anything about big cities, you know that tickets can be anywhere from twenty to one hundred dollars. If you don't pay them, they add up and have additional penalties.

Because I had quite a few added up, I received a notice in the mail. If I didn't pay them, my license was going to be revoked. I needed to see a Justice of the Peace to clear it up. So, I attended the courthouse for a meeting with him to get the fines lowered. The Justice of the Peace I met with was in his sixties. He led me to a room where I sat across from him and presented my tickets. He had to record the conversation while we spoke about the infractions and I plead my case.

When you've had the experiences I have had growing up with a villain, you learn to pay attention to body language as a means of self-preservation. Being in front of this Justice of the Peace, I could feel his eyes all over me in a really dirty and disgusting kind of way. This made me extremely uncomfortable. He directed the conversation and encouraged me to reply in certain ways.

Then he wrapped the conversation up and shut the recorder off. I instantly felt something was up. He told me he could make all the tickets go away if I met with him for coffee. That's all. He stressed how beautiful I was and that he just wanted to speak with me some more. I hesitated and didn't like his suggestion, but my tickets were close to $800 and he didn't give me any other recourse. He said to leave these with him and he would take care of it. I would only need to sign off on one document in a few days for coffee. Reluctantly, I agreed.

What could he do in a public place over coffee? Nothing, right? I called the office in two days, we agreed to meet around the corner from the court offices and we had coffee. I signed the document and that was all. I don't remember all the jibber-jabber of the conversation that we had, but at the end of the conversation, he gave me a small gift bag. I was nervous to open it, but he stressed that I open it there. Inside were some exotic soaps and some other small things.

Soap? He told me that I could use the soap to bathe my body and pay special care to certain parts and think of him. *Yuck,* I thought to myself. There was no way I'd do that. I decided I would give it to the homeless, as soon as possible. I smiled to be polite and said thank you and quickly left. *The end,* I thought. I called the office the next day and was able to confirm my tickets had been wiped clean. I was home free.

A few days later, my phone rang. I answered and was stunned to hear the Justice of the Peace on the other end. Shock rolled over me. I never gave him my phone number. My number was unlisted. How did he get it I asked? He told me he was a Justice of the Peace and could get literally any information he wanted. I told him I couldn't talk that my boyfriend was there and that he was very hostile. I said please don't call back again. I stressed that my boyfriend was the jealous type and had no idea what he would do if he knew a man of any sort was calling my number. It actually wasn't too far from the truth. He wasn't there at that time, but he was really jealous. The Justice of the Peace apologized and I never heard from him again.

Thank goodness. But that scared the crap out of me. From this brief encounter, I learned that nothing is for free. Things could have turned out much worse. I'm glad I escaped with my dignity and a valuable lesson.

Guarded

I dated a prison guard one time who I met at a bar one night. He was such a Casanova with all the ladies around him that night that the name just stuck with him. Cass had an interesting way of making a living and he always had fascinating stories to tell. He was handsome, slightly guarded and still hurting over the end of his last relationship. Cass presented as highly flirtatious, charming, boyish and fun to be around.

After a short period of time dating him, he was acting pretty flippant about what was happening between us so I called it off for a bit. He ended up getting his head straightened around and wanted us to start dating again.

Fast forward to a few months later, things were going well this time around and we decided to live together. I moved to the city he lived in, not far from Belleville. We lived together for only a brief period of time. I really tried to assimilate my life with him. It ended after he got back from holidays one night with one of his best friends. I had been suspicious of his friend for a long time and knew he didn't really like me. In fact, I felt he may have liked my boyfriend as more than just a friend. It was pure speculation and I have never confirmed it or ever asked about it.

It just seemed like their friendship was a little too close for my comfort. I was working two jobs and constantly busy while he was away, making it difficult for him to get a hold of me. Back when cell phones were still very new in the early 90's. When Cass arrived back home, it was quite late. We were happy to see each other, although I was really tired, I opted to go to bed. In bed, we kissed, embraced and chatted when he said he had something he needed to tell me about his trip.

You know that sinking feeling in your stomach, when someone says they need to talk? It's never good when someone says they need to talk. They should just blurt out whatever horrible stuff they have to tell you and be done with it.

Cass told me that he cheated on me—not once—not twice—but three times in the week while he was away. *What?* He cheated on me with a waitress who worked at his friend's restaurant, while he stayed overnight at his house prior to their departure. Then when he was away, he slept with some random woman he met down there. Adding salt to the wound, he then slept with the waitress again when he got back. I was blown away. He said he was sorry, he begged and pleaded with me to forgive him. I calmly got up, packed up my things in a couple of bags and left the apartment in the dead of night. I told him never to talk to me again. I would be back to get the rest of my stuff in a few days and that he was on his own. He didn't just sleep with a random woman on vacation. That might have been washed away in the sands of a vacation tryst.

No, he slept with a waitress, not once, but twice. To add to that, this was a woman he had slept with many times before we ever met. As a kicker, he also confessed to me he might have picked up a sexually transmitted disease while he was away. *Are you kidding me?* The biggest shock to me was that he cheated on me because I wasn't giving him enough sex, and he also couldn't get a hold of me several times while he was away. I was in shock and so angry, I couldn't focus on anything else he said. I grabbed all the stuff I could put in garbage bags and jammed all I could in my car and drove away into the night to stay with my auntie in Belleville.

In the middle of the night I showed up unannounced and told her everything that had happened. I pretty much cried myself to sleep that night from the shame and hurt. In a moment of reprieve, I woke up in the morning to my auntie's loving face and I instantly felt safe and protected by her. I locked my heart back up and put the key in a safe place to be guarded once again by me.

Cass tried numerous times after that to win me back. What Cass did was not only unforgiveable, but deplorable. I made sure I called the waitress to advise her to get checked for a disease, based on his self-report. *Unbelievable.* I had never fully trusted him to start with and I should have gone with my instinct. Trust your instincts. That feeling never lies to you, although it's hard to make sense of sometimes. It is 100 per cent accurate. Believe that.

Chapter 6: BOOMERANG

Boomerang was a very significant man in my life that I met around the time I started dating the private investigator, (Private Eye/P.I.) I was about thirty five. I had just returned from a trip to Ireland and began working at the Shopping Channel.

Bad timing became a theme between us. I'd met him at a trade show. He was charming, and a little older than me. He had all the right words and tons of experience. I had to put the idea of Boomerang on the back burner when I started dating the P.I. Occasionally he would reach out to me and message me to check in with my status and see if I was single.

Boomerang was the first person I called when my relationship with the P.I. took a nosedive. We met for coffee and talked often over the last few weeks of my relationship ending. This did nothing to help my relationship even if there was a chance to fix anything, because I was already interested in someone else. Boomerang and I began to date a little bit after all was said and done with P.I. He wined and dined me like I had always wanted to be. He spoiled me in so many ways and I fell head over heels for him. He offered for me to stay at his place, even though it was still the home he technically shared with his own ex-girlfriend.

Boomerang was on the way out of a bad relationship and there were even pictures of her still around his place on the walls. It was strange, but at the time he offered for me to stay with him and I thought, *why not?* The first night I actually stayed overnight at his house, he told me about his circumstances and I figured it was pretty much over with no hope of recovery. I got a job offer in my hometown around the same time. We got together and I asked him if I should take it.

My auntie was not doing well with the passing of her husband and she was like a mother to me throughout my late teens and onward. I wanted to be there for her and I calculated I could do both. My plan was to stay with her some of the time and alternate with him. It seemed like I had it all worked out. I began my journey between the two cities and stayed with him whenever I was working at The Shopping Channel. I stayed with my auntie while I was working as a morning show host at my hometown radio station.

Throughout the first few months of going back and forth everything seemed fine, but Boomerang had not dissolved his relationship fully and I didn't feel like waiting for the final small details to be wrapped up. I was impatient, and despite all the time we spent together, places we travelled to and romantic moments, it wasn't enough and I didn't want to wait. I ended it.

We remained friends and I would send him the odd message in the months to come on how I was doing. He reached out periodically to see how I was. When I met my Dearly Beloved, I stopped all communication with him at that time.

Scalded by love's pain, I called Boomerang. The man I knew somehow, no matter where he was or what he was doing, he would want to see me. Nor could he resist the temptation to see me again or sleep with me. When I called him he was again with someone at that time. I wanted to see him and talk to him about what had happened in my relationship and get some perspective from an older man. I traveled back to the big city to see him, met him at his condo and had a drink.

While I was there I looked around and saw a picture of another woman by his bed. I asked him if he lived with someone. He said no, but he was seeing someone. I asked why he allowed me to come see him if he was seeing someone. He said, "Because we are friends." *Really?* I thought. His eyes said otherwise. A huge part of me thought, *what the hell am I doing here?*

My heart was so damaged and shredded into pieces that I didn't care about anyone or anything and I ended up in bed with him that night after we returned from dinner. I didn't stay the night, however. We spoke several times after that and he professed how much he loved me and always wanted to be with me "if only I would have some patience for him to get out of another sticky situation." I waited for a bit, but grew tired of this game and once again stopped talking to Boomerang.

A year passed of casual dating after my marriage ended. I had a hurtful and pain-filled year of running from heartache and praying every day that the pain would leave me. I tested my emotional healing process by looking at my wedding photos. I pulled them out once a month and looked through all the pictures of the life I had with my ex-husband. Initially I could barely look at the first one and the tears would roll down my face. I also had a glass of wine in my other hand. Eventually, I would get through a few more pictures without crying. For a long time, I would cry and cry and cry over those pictures. So devastated, more so than I ever had been in my life.

Then I met my prince and I checked that piece of my heart that belonged to my ex-husband in a box. I focused all my love and energy on my prince until that ended too. Who do you suppose I immediately call when it all finally blew up and it was over? You guessed it, Boomerang. I called him, I cried to him, I went to see him and we spent some time together once again. It was brief, because, yet again, he was with someone. Jeesh, how bad was our timing?

How could this guy and I never manage to get together when we were either single, or not coming in and out of a relationship? He professed his love for me again, told me how he wanted to marry me, how he wanted to have a baby with me and a bunch of crazy stuff. All of this I took in and thought, *how can this be?* He was living with someone else, had bought a house with her, but it was in her name for business reasons. More of how they got together and where he was at came out in the few weeks that we spoke after our initial get together. I always run to Boomerang after a breakup, cry to him and sleep with him and it never worked out.

Why did I keep doing this? It's insanity. This guy and I were never meant to be. Nothing made sense anymore and I couldn't do this back and forth thing with him any longer. Once again, he wanted me to be patient so he could get out of his situation so he could be with me. I was pissed. I let it go for a few weeks and tried to understand. We talked on the phone several times and he constantly stroked this idea of us two being together, but he needed some time. He said he was in a complicated situation and a lot of money was at stake. What kind of idiot did he think I was? I wasn't waiting around for him and I was pretty upset that he wanted me to, again.

If he loved me so much and wanted to be with me so bad, he wouldn't have cared about that girl and would have cared more about me. My ego said to let go of the idea once and for all and move on. I stopped talking with him after I gave him a piece of my mind. He contested my views on all of it and told me I would regret my decision. I haven't regretted it. We knew each other for close to ten years and you can only do this dance for so long till your legs grow tired and you become bored by the same old song and dance. We spoke a couple of times since then, as friends. My goal was to remain neutral with him and have no harsh feelings. Trying to take the high road is never easy, but it makes you feel a lot better in the end.

Chapter 7: MY DEARLY BELOVED ALL STAR

When you tell a good love story, there always has to be a blossoming romance in it and all my love stories start off so amazingly. Don't all romances? I would never get involved with someone if there were not some seriously intense emotions to propel me past my fear of love and of being alone. It is a terrible dance I seem to have been doing forever. My last romance ended so terribly that I thought that was it for me.

I had just ended a year and a half relationship with a P.I. Our relationship fizzled out because I thought he would never love me the way that he loved his first wife. I would never be his true love, I would just be a new love. You will read more about him in my busted chapter.

Needless to say, I left that situation and stayed with Boomerang while I worked at The Shopping Channel. Not to sound fickle, my reasoning for this decision was that he lived near my job at the time. I asked if I could stay there as I had nowhere else to go except at another girlfriend's house. I bounced back and forth from hers to his when I could. It was a temporary fix.

In this chaotic time of my life, I was thrilled when I got a call from my now co-host on the morning radio show, who asked if I would come work at the station. I was in work/escape mode and thought, why not go back and forth between both jobs since the new job offer was in my home town?

My thoughts also turned to my auntie, who is like a mother to me. Her husband, (my uncle,) had died months earlier and she was struggling with her grief. She had always been there for me and I wanted to return the love and support. So, I took the job, lived with her, stayed at my friend's house and Boomerang's occasionally all while I began a wheel of work. I ended up doing this for a year and a half before I had to make some changes.

Boomerang was at the end of a breakup. I was in transit and we decided it wasn't a good time for us to try and make romance work. I went on a few dates with others in the city, until the fateful day I met my future husband. From the very moment I saw him, I knew I wanted to be with him, and that we would be together.

Every year the United Way has a big event that involved dancing. It's an event where they pair up different celebrity types and big names in the community to practice and perform in a big venue.

I had been living back in my hometown of Belleville for about six months when this opportunity came up in March, 2010. It was with that opportunity that I met my husband the All Star. He was all of that and more. In a quest to start his own business, he had just returned to his hometown. We weren't paired up for the event. Instead, I was partnered with one of my colleagues, a popular radio jock and musical performer. By now, you must be wondering how we got together.

The All Star had a meet-and-greet for the contestants at his bar where I first laid eyes on him. His charisma and stunning confidence made me smile. With my professional hat on, I approached each of the duos. I asked them to come on our radio station and give the listeners some background on them. Before any big event, it's always good business to build some hype in the few months ahead. Drawn like a magnet, I approached him first. As a sentiment of that beginning, I still have the photo of when he first came into the studio with his dance partner. We had already exchanged numbers at the meet-and-greet to co-ordinate the radio interviews.

As I look back, it really was an unexpected romance. He was nine years younger than me, I had just turned thirty-eight and he was twenty-nine, but I couldn't get over how confident he was. We got engaged a year and a half after we met. The total of our incredible time together was two and a half years. To think about it, that was a far cry from my usual six months. It was a whirlwind romance and everything felt like it was falling into place so perfectly. I thought, this is the feeling I have been waiting for. The sweetest moment was when he asked me to marry him.

To paint the picture of that moment he asked me to marry him, I was in the bathroom getting ready for work, and his beautiful dog was in the bedroom. My All Star was settling down after just getting home from a long night at the bar. I was always up quite early and sometimes his nights ran late. With this schedule, our paths would cross from time-to-time when on occasion, we would be awake at the same time.

Almost ready, I went into our room and sat on the bed. We talked about the night and how it went, he shared that he was stressed. I never liked to see him stressed and would always do my best to try and fix his worries. My All Star stood up all of a sudden, went to his dresser and returned with something in his hand. As he came toward me, everything else kind of slipped away. He got down on one knee with the dog right beside him, and asked me to marry him with his grandmother's ring. To say I was overwhelmed would be an understatement. I never saw it coming. Not even the slightest hints some girls pick up on. I later learned he had the ring awhile and wanted to surprise me. Surprise me, he most certainly did. I felt honored to wear his grandmother's ring and it was the perfect choice.

I had to rush off to work. He came with me, and we called his mother on radio and let her know the amazing news. His parents were amazing people and always so kind to me. They made me believe in the truest sense of family in the way they always supported each other. No matter what, they always had one another's back. I was so in love with him and his family.

Life couldn't be more perfect at this point. We immediately set a date for the upcoming month of September. Just under a year from when he asked me. The task of selecting everything was left to his mother and I for the most part and she helped me immensely. His mother was a selfless woman who always put her family first. I would do anything for this family, too.

During our time together, he helped me get over so many issues I had acquired growing up. He helped me conquer my fear of water. With his support and encouragement, I took up wakeboarding, one of the activities he loved to do so much. Despite the villain's numerous attempts to drown me growing up, my love for the All Star far outweighed my fear of the water and I was willing to try and overcome that fear that had lived with me so long.

I remember driving out to the Wakeboard School and having a mini panic attack thinking of being in the water and going under the water. The whole way my All Star comforted me and talked me down. He was so supportive and he really wanted me to try. My heart was still palpitating, even on the boat. I needed to see what I was going to do to be prepared. I ended up going first and shook like a leaf in the water. I never told the All Star why I was so scared. I wanted to be brave and I just stayed focused on him in the boat smiling and encouraging me that I could do this.

The life jacket I had on definitely helped ease my fear, even though it didn't deter the memories from flooding in when I was out there floating in the water. Memories of the times I had been learning to swim crashed to the surface. The villain became infuriated with me because I wasn't doing it the right way he wanted. As I felt the cool water around me floating with the wakeboard strapped to my feet, I thought of what would happen when I wiped out and I went under the water.

Would I be ok? Being under the water was terrifying for me. As a kid, the villain's solution for errors in my swimming lessons with him was to hold me under the water until I struggled for air. The villain's sick way of forcing me to try harder to do what he wanted me to and often times, he just made me unravel and feel worse. It was harder to learn to swim with this fear so engrained in me. On a few occasions I struggled so much for air that I thought I was going to die. He coldly looked at me and used his hands to force me down under the water.

Despite all of that, my love for the All Star conquered the aftermath of the villain. I also developed a love of the snow and snowboarding while I was with him, too. He was incredible at both sports and I always marveled at his natural athletic ability. I admired it and I loved seeing him in his true element. My admiration for his skills inspired me to learn how to snowboard. Not easily though, as I hadn't been on skis before. The fact that I detested the cold didn't help. Thanks to yet another remnant involving the villain and his wrath in my earlier life. I had managed to avoid even owning a pair of snow boots my entire life right up until I met my All Star. I hated the cold that much and avoided being outside too long at all costs.

When I was only twelve-years-old, I spent an entire day out in the freezing cold. My dislike grew from that cold winter day. I had been home and it had snowed quite heavily the night before. I had been outside, shoveled the snow from the driveway, and had cleaned the car off that the villain usually used. However, he was angry that I didn't clean the other car off that he hardly ever used. I had no idea what prompted him to come in that day and grab me by my hair and drag me down a flight of stairs and out the back door.

His hold on me was tight and he grabbed me by my collar as he flung me across the frozen pool without letting go of me. He dragged me to where the car was still covered in snow and demanded I clean it off. I had to stand outside all day until my mother came home that evening as a lesson to me to never do that again. I stood for hours outside in my Michael Jackson three quarter length t-shirt, jeans, and socks. He offered that day, if I were to please him sexually, then I could come back inside. I had been given a choice for the first time in all the years he had been abusing me. Guess what? I chose to freeze.

The heat from my rebellion kept me focused while I slowly lost feeling in my toes. As the rest of my body shivered, I drew my strength from within and prayed I would be able to make it till the afternoon. My mother finally came home to find me shivering in the cold. She asked why I was outside with no coat or shoes on. I told her and she shook her head and told me to follow her in. It was one of the few times that I was ever happy to see my mother. That memory stayed with me forever, but then one day love made my fears melt away.

This sharing of my trauma may seem scattered or misplaced

when reading about my All Star, but the truth is, in the wake of long-standing trauma, this is how my brain works. With whatever bliss I experience, it is always laced with memories I have to navigate through. The scars from my abuse impact every waking moment of my life, as it does for most survivors. Although this piece may seem misplaced, I believe it's important to show you how someone with a history of trauma relates to the world. With every joyous moment, it's measured against the bad ones. We never escape it, but sometimes, just sometimes, we can learn to persevere in spite of it and reconstruct a new template for living.

The All Star made me believe that the snow was good and fun. I prepared myself to learn snowboarding at the age of forty and learned to wakeboard at thirty-nine. You're never too old to learn something that is for sure! I thought learning to snowboard would require a lot of falling so I wore roller blading gear under my clothes and out I went.

We snowboarded locally and travelled all over Ontario and Quebec as I conquered my past and created new and beautiful memories. I took lesson after lesson and practiced and practiced. As a side note, I highly recommend tailbone protector pants if you ever decide to learn to snowboard. It will save you a thousand tears and help prevent a bruised tailbone in the process. Poor All Star hung in there with me. So often, at the end of many runs, I would be in tears from falling. But I got up, every single time...over and over again.

Often my All Star would be at the bottom of the run waiting for me to come down, praying that I wasn't crying. He cheered me on when I made it down the run without falling. Eventually, I mastered my fear and distaste for the snow. I also managed to develop my skills at my new-found sport. I do admit, it took lots of practice. I tackled the fear with him and he was a great supporter of it all. I did it all for love.

Being beside the All Star was where I always wanted to be. In the beginning of our dating, his business had a real struggle to get going. It had suffered an unfortunate fire and that really brought him down, but not out. I remember the night he found out that it had caught fire and he was devastated. At the time I was working in between The Shopping Channel and my gig as a Morning Radio Host. Although I was jam-packed with work, I remained at his side the whole way. Just like he supported me through my traumas and fears, I stuck with him, ensuring he would get through it with any help I could provide.

At the time I still lived with my auntie at her place, and she divided her time between St. Catharines and Belleville. She had met a nice man on a trip we went on together. Everything was coming together so nicely for her and I was so happy.

You see, on a happy side note, my auntie had not been on a vacation ever in her life and I had convinced her to go on a work vacation trip that happens every year. I thought this might help lift her spirits after my uncle's passing almost seven months before.

This trip to Jamaica turned out to be life-changing for her. On the plane ride down there, we sat next to each other and she was a little nervous. I was my usual self and talked to everyone around me, even an elderly man next to me. However, his much younger girlfriend at the time, (I didn't know was his girlfriend,) was sitting on the other aisle and apparently didn't like my chatter.

A couple of hours passed by and I grew tired of her razor glares and looked behind me to see an empty seat. I decided to sit there. The man the seat belonged to came out of the washroom. Being me, and determined, I told him his new seat was up there and pointed to the empty seat next to my Auntie. He was pretty easy going and said sure. The two sat next to each other the whole way down and were giggling and laughing the whole way. She found out his wife had passed away a few months prior from cancer too. They had a lot in common. By the time we got off the plane, they were positively smitten with one another.

Fast forward–they ended up together! She divided her time between the two cities for a little while and eventually moved in with him. When Auntie was in St Catharines, I didn't want to stay there all alone in the house, so I moved in with the All Star into his place. The blending of our belongings created a lovely home together. I finally had a reason to rescue my beautiful furniture and home items from storage. I eventually made a decision to give up my television career to help him focus on his business and grow into something much greater than before. He had great ambition. Coupled with some much needed help and guidance, I knew it would be a great success for him. He had a vision, and I wanted to help him grow it to what he always wanted it to be.

Everything from colors of the wall, decor, to organizing the layout and making do with what he had, we worked together on it all. I helped with the bar marketing, menu planning and structuring the ads for the radio. It was a real team effort. From the bottom up we worked tirelessly on it all. We spent a lot of time together and molded his dream into an attractive business and clientele.

The time I devoted to my All Star to help make his dreams come true included sacrificing some of my career aspirations, which I gladly did. This made me feel real love for him on an even deeper and more meaningful level. I felt he loved me so and we did everything together. We travelled, held parties, attended family gatherings, had special celebrations with friends and worked side by side every day. I gained immense confidence in my ability to maintain composure during stressful times working his bar business. I learned that I could selflessly love someone and make their dreams a part of my own dreams, too. I could see what he aspired to and I could see how I could help him. I'm always driven by a deep desire to help those I love.

Two and a half years went by so quickly and when our wedding came around there was even more to deal with as he had acquired a second business. That's when I noticed how much less we saw of each other. Our time was divided between two places of work and the time we spent apart took its toll on us. I missed him terribly, but we sacrificed our quality time for the pursuit of a long-term future together. Shortly after we got married, everything fell apart. The demands of two businesses overran the foundation of our relationship. We didn't see each other if at all during the summer of our marriage and a great many other things crushed our love into tiny bits. When you don't spend quality time together, and argue all the time over this and that, you slowly drift apart.

Pretty soon we were only fighting and rarely saw each other. I completely fell apart. The life we built together, the dreams we pursued, faded to black. Every day my heart darkened more and more. All that sunshine of the summer was bleak and miserable in my life at that time. It was the worst summer of my life.

This is where I have to end this part of my story for All Star. After it's all said and done, it doesn't matter the finite details of why it ended. There are some things you can't justify making public, so I will keep my thoughts to myself in this regard. The only two people who know why it ended are he and I. The legally wed part was brief—only three months, but what can you do? The mark of this relationship for me was one of great healing, yet it ended with great sorrow. I choose to remember the good, because there was so much of it in our relationship. Only the ending was bad.

It hurt to lose my best friend and a beautiful family. It hurt to put so much of my heart, soul and life into something and for it all to be taken away. I never thought we would ever be apart. I married him because I had waited forever to find that perfect someone and I thought he was the one. We were so close for so long and shared so much together, that I choose to remember the man I married as one that I was madly in love with. I would have never gotten married otherwise.

He was my All Star and he was my husband. He will always be my first husband and probably my last. At this point in my life, I think I can safely say I don't want to get married ever again. I never want to face the humiliation of it failing in front of everyone again. I thought at the age of forty that I would only get married once. I waited and waited for the right one to come along. Regardless of the good and the healing of so many of my scars I managed to get from it, I don't think I will ever have that kind of deep-rooted faith in someone again. My heart is not fragile, but the very thought of loving this hard and falling again is more than I can bear.

You would think that after feeling utter and total heartbreak from my separation and soon-to-be-divorce that I would have just evaporated into thin air, but I didn't. I wanted to. I could feel my heart beating inside of me, although I couldn't feel any love in my heart anymore. It had grown incredibly cold inside and I was sure that it would never feel the love I had felt when I was with the All Star. I knew I had to pick myself up and keep going.

Chapter 8 - THE LEGEND

A mere one week after the formal conclusion of my marriage, I was back to the grindstone. I forced myself to work through tears and kept my head above water. At my radio gig, I cried in between breaks and tried and keep myself together. My colleague and friend at work encouraged me daily to keep going. Who else was going to help me keep going? I had to summon my strength from within and remind myself that I had been through much worse in life, just not the painful heartache that I had just experienced. This was new to me, but I knew I had to press on.

My birthday was on the horizon just weeks after the breakup. One of my cousins, Cub, who I'm so close with, invited me to visit her in Ottawa. She encouraged me to not spend my birthday alone. So, I did what every woman does to make herself feel better. I bought an expensive dress and got my hair all done up nice to go see her. My cousin was in her mid-twenties at the time and literally one of the most outgoing young women I know. She reminds me of myself sometimes when I was her age, yet she is a lot more even-keeled that I ever was.

Cub planned a night out where we visited a few of the hot spots in her city with her girlfriends to cheer me up. Just as I expected, we had a great time and then some. She knows how to enjoy life. Everyone in the core of the city pretty much knew who she was, having worked at so many different places.

The night of my birthday, we got all dolled up, indulged in some drinks and made our way around to some bars. One seriously happening bar was on their list to visit, because the guys and the girls that worked there were undeniably good looking. Some even ridiculously good looking. One guy in particular was jaw-dropping-hot. I never reveal to anyone I'm intensely attracted to that I find them appealing. I play my cards really, really close to me. Most handsome guys are used to women falling all over them. I refuse to be one of those girls. In fact, I'll often work harder to ignore them.

Legend, is what I chose to name him. It's a nickname the young girls called him. He was a legend at that bar. All who attended it remembered him for many reasons. In just about every single way, this guy was perfect. Tall, fit, handsome, great smile, super sexy and he was a pretty damn good bartender too. As soon as Cub's posse of ladies and I made our way into the bar, they all were overjoyed that Legend was working. They squealed with delight for me. They hoped he'd be there so I could see this hottie. Legend worked the crowd like nobody's business.

Behind the bar, he was so upbeat and friendly with his fellow staff while he worked the ladies on the other side. Pretty soon, Legend made his way down to our end of the bar and he started to get our drink orders. Our eyes met and I held his gaze long enough to indicate my attraction.

Legend served up our drinks with a smile and the girls beckoned him to concoct one of his "special" shots for me. In fact, the girls insisted on it. He obliged and what happened next, I was totally unprepared for. Legend whipped up this shooter called a Muffdiver.

He then hopped up on the bar counter facing me with his jeans all snugged up in all the right places.

My cheeks burned with embarrassment, I must have been so red in the face. I giggled uncontrollably. I was puzzled beyond belief when he placed a martini glass filled with what appeared to be whip cream between his legs. I looked around at the girls to find out what the heck I was supposed to do next. I had to put my hands behind my back and take the shot out of the martini glass with my mouth. *What?* I just had my hair done and I was dressed to the nines. I didn't want to get whip cream in my hair and I did NOT want to put my face in this guy's crotch.

In retrospect, I probably should have wanted to because every other girl in the bar paid him to do the same shot with them. Legend stared down at me with those big, sexy eyes and I put my hands behind my back and moved my hair to one side. As I shifted my body toward this mound of cream, I quickly averted the plan, picked it up with my hands and tossed the shot back. The look on Legends face was priceless, it was pure surprise before a huge grin overtook his face.

Nobody had ever done that before to him, according to Legend. I was happy to be among the few, if any who had not obliged this kind of shot in the way that it was intended.

At the time the shot was delivered, Cub was in the bathroom and upon returning to the crew was very upset that she did not get to see the shot go down. She was in stitches when she heard what I did and insisted that I get another shot delivered by Legend. Cub ordered it and before I knew it, Legend was back in front of me, tight jeans and whip cream. *Here we go again,* I thought. I had already made my mind up that I still wasn't going to take a shot out of a glass in some hot guy's crotch, or anyone's for that matter. It's just not my style. From the eyes we had been giving each other, I estimated my rewards would be greater if I didn't follow the norm he'd come to expect of swooning women. Round two ended the same way and even more gasps came from the crowd. By that time, Legend was not only laughing, but from his constant glances and engaging smiles, I could tell he was intrigued.

The night went on, we all danced, drank and socialized with the crowd together. I initiated occasional eye contact in hopes to relay my interest in him. The consistent return of glances and smiles suggested to me he may just be into me, too. At one point of the night the bartenders lit the bar on fire and really got the crowd going. It was such entertainment and fantastic fun on a night I needed more distraction than ever from my broken heart. Legend made it even better.

As we began to get ourselves together to head out for the night, Legend took a moment to give me his phone number. Finally back at Cub's house, I was a little tipsy. With my inhibitions lowered, irrational thoughts flooded in. My most forward thought was to shed myself of this broken heart and the only way to get over someone was to get under someone. I texted Legend and agreed to meet up with him in the early hours of the morning.

My cousin was furious and protective over me. She didn't want me to go anywhere. At that point though, my self-esteem and heart had been so crushed, her pleas fell on deaf ears. We actually got into a disagreement before I left. I wasn't sure exactly where I was going to go, but I was definitely going to seal the end of this night with a kiss from his lips. I left despite my cousin's requests and met Legend outside her place.

Lucky in Love

My cousin is an amazing person and I never like to argue with her. The over protectiveness that night was warranted, as I wear my heart on my sleeve. Sometimes I put others wants, needs and desires above my own. This wasn't the case for this particular situation, as I saw it. It was my needs, desires and wants that ruled my head and other parts of my body. I craved distraction from the immense pain of my shattered heart that night.

We decided to hang out in my car which led to becoming lip-locked and entangled within seconds of closing the doors. All that tension between us through the night came rushing forward, despite my lingering pain. The devastation from the last breakup slipped away a little more with every kiss. Legend lived up to his name, his kisses were powerful and his arms even more so. You know that saying, he knew how to kiss me? Boy did he ever. Things heated up quickly in the car between us. Hands all over each other's bodies, we indulged in groping, and grabbing and lusted after one another.

Legend was every bit of what everyone attested to him to be, and then some. However, things would only go so far between us in a car. Pretty soon the steam had to die down and reality asserted itself that "it" was not going to happen tonight. Nonetheless, Legend was just the right prescription for someone trying to mend a broken heart. We spoke a few times after that and tried to arrange a time or a date that we could hang out again, but life moves fast and too much time had lagged on. We never saw each other again. Every time someone orders a Muffdiver shot at a bar though, I think of him and smile. True legends never die.

***

Soon after Legend, I began a stream of frivolous dates. One week here, and two weeks there with whoever crossed my path for whatever reason. I gravitated towards whoever I fancied for whatever purpose or reason. My only goal at that time was to try anything to take the pain away and distract me from what I was feeling inside. I drank wine with my friends and dated casually until one day, I couldn't cope that way anymore. I decided I was ready to get over this.

Throughout the next year, I looked at my wedding photographs and pictures from my life with All-Star and I cried every time. As the months moved along, I opened up the pictures and tested my emotions and progress with getting over what had happened. I cried less each time, until I finally I decided that I didn't want to look at them anymore. At that point, I put them away for good. I had to get over this and move past the pain and the humiliation. After all, I waited forever to get married and then when I did, it blew up in three months.

I found the experience so embarrassing. It happened in front of everyone in my hometown. Nonetheless, an image resonated with me one day while driving around the city. I spotted a billboard with a very fit woman on it. It was a before and after picture. In her before picture, she looked much bigger than I felt at that time, and she was incredibly fit after. I felt a surge of connection to that woman on that billboard and I realized what I wanted to do with all the pain that had collected inside me. I wanted to weight train and build my body into a strong physique.

Most importantly, I wanted to feel strong inside again. I desperately wanted to feel alive. One of my girlfriends told me I had "back fat" the last time we were at the beach. That comment came on the heels of how I already realized my days of wining and dining had come with a price. I could no longer deny it. I embarked on a fitness journey that would literally change my life. I called the owner of Body by Sergio and we set to the task of making my fitness goals a reality. To my delight, we reached them in less than six months. I saw changes in my body even earlier than that.

Each week we trained, I cried, some from the pain of training and other tears fell from the emotional pain and trauma I shed from my childhood. With every curl, push up and repetition, I felt all that pain and humiliation of my failed marriage slip away. Later the next year, I appeared on the billboard too and the following year as well. Just like the woman I had seen on the billboard a year prior, there I was on it, with my own before and after and my own story. I turned my life around, learned to love myself again and felt empowered more than ever. That's when I would meet the man I thought was my Prince.

Chapter 9: THE PRINCE OR THE JESTER?

Some seriously necessary reflection led me to begin this chapter at the point of my brief escape to British Columbia. I took a much needed break at my dear friend Liesa's place. What a serene and peaceful place to be. I had been promising her forever that I would come visit her. It had been six years since we last saw each other. As fate would have it, I had no idea when I booked the trip months ago that my Prince and I would split. This is where I put pen to paper to purge my next heartbreak.

Even though this is a perfect place for me to write about him, I'm going to cry writing this. I can feel the tears already welling up inside my eyes, so I pour a Grey Goose Vodka and soda to at least soothe my soul as I write.

The Prince arrived in my life when I felt I was clear from my ex-husband's departure. It had been over a year. The sad thing for me now, is I realize I didn't take enough time alone to heal from the pain that had been caused by the All Star. I moved out of our marital home abruptly. In fact, the strength I used to leave propelled me forward with such a force, I believed I was ok when I had stopped crying all the time. I moved into my own place, but in hindsight, I didn't spend enough time alone.

If I had taken the healthy, rational route for emotional recovery, it would have meant committing to a period with no men at all in my life. In all honesty, it's been my experience that as soon as I say that, more men appear. It was difficult for me to stick to the healthier way then, because the pain was so immense. I guess in order to keep my life together I used the casual hook-ups to keep me functioning and feeling better than I actually was. I was afraid that if I became totally void of men, I would drown in the pain and I couldn't allow myself to do that. Little did I know, that eventually we all have to face the pain and that you can't run forever. Which is why I am here now, writing this chapter while my Prince Charming is no longer in my life.

My sweet Prince Charming came gallantly into my life at one of my sister's thirtieth birthday party. I wanted to plan this party for my littlest sister, as we had not been in one another's lives growing up and I had only recently become reacquainted with her. I have three siblings from my father, two girls from one woman and one boy from another who is seven months older than me. I have another sister, who I grew up with from my biological mother and the villain. I invited friends of hers and colleagues from her work, which ironically included the Prince's sister-in-law, little did I know.

The party began, the DJ had the music pumping after a beautiful dinner and other people arrived to celebrate her big day. Newly single again, I was able to focus on my sister and her guests without the stress of relationship woes weighing me down. I had been chatting to a few of them when I heard more come in. As I turned around, there stood this incredibly tall, athletic and handsome man. His smile beamed so big at me and I had to step back to take him all in. The appearance of this man brought me back to that adolescent moment of swooning. I found myself giddy, in awe, and a little unsure.

My cheeks burned, my pulse raced and I was totally

overwhelmed by his unmistakable presence. The room around us melted away and all I could see was him. The music faded out of my ears and it felt like it was just the two of us. It seemed like there was nobody else around. For a good thirty minutes, I couldn't pull myself away from him for fear that the Prince would disappear. I was so giddy, I had to excuse myself finally to go to the bathroom and have a heart to heart with my inner-adolescent in the mirror.

Orlena, I said. *Pull it together, you're all soft, vulnerable and acting like a young girl right now. You need to be more casual and confident.* I couldn't let him see the foolish hope that lingered behind my smile. I couldn't let him know that I was a staggering fool for love. Upon my return to the soiree, I took to the dance floor with my sister. It was impossible to resist the need to keep my eye on him. Our exchanging glances and smiles could easily be seen as a courting dance. Through my dancing, smiling and gyrating around the dance floor with some girls and my sister, I maintained eye contact every chance I could. I wasn't on the dance floor for more than ten minutes when another girl approached him. She smiled at him and showed him her phone.

Something inside me sparked the urge to pay special attention to this man, and the potential competition. The next short song, I headed back toward him and casually asked who the girl was. I didn't recognize her and had to remember inviting her. She was a guest of a guest and had proceeded to show him some boudoir photos of her on her phone. This blatant move would clearly indicate to him that if I ended up being a no, that she was a definite yes.

You can't blame a girl for trying, but he was looking for his princess and not a pin-up girl. She did this right in front of me with no sign of consideration I had been talking to him for a half an hour.

This woman showed even less regard for the fact that it was my sister's birthday party. How rude! That would be like walking into someone's house and helping yourself to their fine china. Jeesh! I definitely wasn't her biggest fan.

The night wrapped up and I hadn't taken a single drink. He, his sister-in-law, her husband and his brother, wanted to head home. I jumped at the chance to chauffeur, not thinking really or caring how I was going to get back to my car and my home. Something inside me didn't want to leave this beautiful man's side. Instead of a big white horse, this Prince Charming drove a big black Escalade. I was a tiny doll behind the wheel and he laughed at how small I was compared to him. That I liked even more. His personality and his size enveloped me and created feelings of safety and security.

We drove to his brother's house and it was quite late. The instant connection grew into something beautiful. We cuddled on his brother's chaise lounge and the incredible sense I belonged in his arms resonated with me. I was so comfortable and felt so safe that I ended up staying over and had to wear a t-shirt to cuddle up next to him. Nothing happened between us that night. Maybe that was why I fell for his charismatic and gentlemanly behavior. His kiss was like butter on my lips and I had never felt that luxurious sensual bliss ever.

It was like I always imagined the perfect kiss to be. Not too much mush, and not too much force. It seemed My Prince offered the perfect combination of passion and persuasion. The warmth and security of his powerful arms around me were intoxicating like a drug, I fell asleep peacefully. When I awoke in the morning, I thought *oh boy, here we go. What do I say and how do I act now that the love potion of the night had worn off? Or had it?* No it had not.

It was still present, I gazed into his big, crystal blue eyes and fell for him even more. I knew at that moment, I was going to fall madly in love with him. Prince Charming struck me as the perfect guy. His sense of humor, his wit, his tenderness and the sincerity in his touch and his gaze made me believe I would be safe with him. We got up that morning fairly early and had some coffee with his sister-in-law and brother. Everything seemed so natural between us in the morning. The comfort level was as though we had been together for months. He admitted to me later, that he saw me on his sister-in-law's Facebook page.

My Prince shared his belief that if he had some time with me, we would get along well. He was right, there was incredible chemistry between us. The only thing that spoiled the moment was the ticking clock. The day was moving on, with or without us. We grabbed my car and headed back to my place. There, we talked more about how he ended up in Belleville. The Prince had also lived there when he was nineteen. As he was a year younger than me, I had left my hometown around the time he was here.

My Prince shared what had brought him to the party where we crossed paths. He had been around for a funeral the night before that he hadn't planned to attend. They had drinks and even got tattoos that day. *What a rush of events,* I thought. His son was in town with him and staying at his aunt and uncle's which was not far from where we were at that time. Everything seemed to fit so well together.

Back at my place after breakfast, we indulged in some harmless rolling around and heavy kissing before he left, but we still hadn't taken that next step. By the time he'd left, that's all I could think about. *The next step. When would be the next time I would see the Prince?* We had each other's phone numbers and we communicated by text and by phone over the next week or so. I needed to see him again to ensure myself that it was not a temporary spell that we were under. I needed to confirm it was a real feeling between the two of us. I wasn't sure of what it was still, but I couldn't wait much longer. Not knowing haunted me daily.

When I saw him next, we had arranged a weekend in the city where he lived so it was more convenient for him. That particular weekend was a busy one. There was a major hockey tournament in town and there were no available hotels anywhere to be found that suited my preferences. We had agreed that I wouldn't stay at his house as he had his children there that weekend and we wanted to wait to see what would progress between us before he would introduce me to them.

Time was not a luxury for him and I wasn't sure how much we would be able to spend with each other anyway. Prince Charming never really had any time to himself. His marriage had ended the same time as mine had, more than a year before and he now had his fifteen-year-old son with him full time and his twins every other weekend.

Hockey schedules had him running ragged and there wasn't much time for just him. Not only was this a fully booked weekend with hockey tournaments but it was also a busy weekend for him at his house too. He was going to get away for a little while to see me. I arrived in his city with the idea I would book a hotel room there and that it would be no problem at all...I was wrong. The hotels were all booked up except for some of the shoddiest ones around. The one I had found, I figured wouldn't be so bad based on the level that the hotel was in other cities...I was wrong again. It was terrible. I agreed to meet him there after speaking with him on the phone. I had wine and some snacks, but even the expensive wine wouldn't make this room any better. It really didn't matter to me as I desperately wanted to kiss him again. If for no other reason than to check and see if I was right about him.

I had no idea if we were going to take our relationship to the next level that night, but I definitely knew I was open to the possibility at this point. When I walked into the room, I gasped. There were two double beds. It was a small room with the worst selection in bedding I had seen. It looked like I had stepped back into the seventies and I called to quickly warn him. Dare I compare it to the infamous Bates Motel? This was not to my standard by any stretch of the imagination, but what choice did I have?

Thankfully, we both laughed at the sight of it and relief washed over me. Here we were, in the most hideous motel room possible, yet we were entirely smitten with each other and didn't care what the room looked like. To make the night memorable, I wrote a sweet note on a shoddy piece of paper I found on the hotel table that said something to the effect that *this was the beginning of something beautiful and that the journey would be one to discover together.* I kept the note forever as a reminder of our love.

The Prince and I fell madly in love with each other after that. In the beginning, I had spent a weekend in Montreal with one of my cousins. I saw my favorite team play, met all the players after the game and had even got invited out that night with one of the players. The invite was extended for breakfast the next day and I didn't blink an eye to turn it down. My thoughts only consisted of the Prince. Even my favorite hockey team couldn't sway me from the object of my affection. I thought of his kiss, his smile, his arms around me and how completely amazing I felt when I was with him. From the end of one visit to the next, time dragged on for me. I just wanted to be around him again.

The very next day after the game, I dropped my cousin off in Ottawa where she was attending University. I proceeded to drive across Ontario from Quebec to be with him almost seven hours away. I even took a spare day off work, which I rarely ever do, just so I could spend more time with him. I was crazy about him. My Prince had completely captivated me. I stayed with him at his house. That is when I caught a glimpse of just how much my Prince was in need of a Princess. Actually, he was in need of a maid for sure...and in time I would realize he also needed more than that. He needed an accountant, a time manager and oh so much more. His castle was sparse, his possessions few and his laundry abundant. It was everywhere, and I do mean everywhere.

Come to think of it, he did have a maid to try and keep up with it all, but I could tell this guy was running for his life. It was crystal clear to me how much I could complement his life with the skills I had to offer. My organizing, home making and knack of making a house a home would be a huge asset to him and his life. We met in November. At Christmas time, I brought all my decorations to his house, and even bought more just so he could have a real Christmas celebration in his home with his children. I wanted him to be comforted with love. I wanted him to feel peace. I did loads of laundry when I came to visit on the weekends and I cooked for his children. I went to their hockey games and I listened to how awful things had been for him when he and his ex split up.

How unfairly he had been treated, I thought, and I fell even more for him, because I understood how it felt to be mistreated. To be used up, and to be left with your heart scattered in pieces all around. I wanted to help nourish his strength back to where he would thrive again. I felt that by giving that sacred part of me, I would receive it in return. It's said it's better to give than to receive right? Time moved by so quickly between the weeks we got to know each other. We would count the days from the last weekend to the next one.

Three months after we met, we decided that we would buy a house together and figure out later how we would actually be able to live together in it. The concept of him bringing his children to Belleville and staying in my one bedroom apartment wasn't going to work long-term. So we needed to figure something out. Yes, I know, it probably wasn't the smartest thing to do. I didn't care. I followed what I felt was the best thing to do. In fact, he wasn't sure he would even be able to leave his city at all due to his job.

We decided he would commute to see me and that I would move in and at least we would have a house in my city and in his. Summer came, along with an unfortunate job loss for him. It forced him to look for work elsewhere and that was hard. I believed it was a blessing in disguise, because we could be together maybe in my city. He eventually sold his house, moved into our home together and began to look for work. Over time, with the help of a girlfriend who lived with us, and we had a tenant downstairs renting in an apartment; we managed to make it through some tough times.

His ex was relentless. We never met and we never talked to each other. She continued to make his life as difficult as she could and it weighed heavily on our relationship. It was awful to say the least, and it took a toll on us and it hurt us in many ways. We loved each other through the very worst of it, but it wasn't easy.

The abandonment he felt, coupled with my own issues would make for a horrible dance of insecurity between us. I know that we both had a subtle fear that the other would leave, which is maybe why we jumped right into things. Both of us were still reeling from our failed marriages for whatever reasons they ended. Neither of us chose to end them, and therein lay some of our problems. Jumping into things without thinking is not a good idea. You really do need to get to know someone and make sure you get along together and ensure that things can be cohesive. If you have different ways of doing things, life can become a series of debates over what to do and how to do it. That can wear on your love.

There were glimmers of these insecurities in his constant need for attention throughout our relationship. One thing I've always known about myself is that I have a big personality, a healthy dose of ego and I don't like to cater to a man's ego outside of simple daily compliments. I felt the amount you give out in the beginning of a relationship, is not always sustainable. I found that was what he needed most from me. We moved forward in our relationship quickly. We immersed ourselves into every aspect of our lives. Whatever dream or vision I had, he wanted to be part of it and it gave his life meaning to be. I felt the same way. We would talk about what each other wanted and we would always try and make one another happy.

The presence in one another's lives made a lot of our issues disappear for the most part or at least subside for a while. I had no idea that we would have so much to deal with in the aftermath and wreckage of each other's lives. With every event he went to, with every trip we took together, every birthday party we celebrated for his children, new life was breathed into our relationship. Every special holiday or summer vacation we took, we built memories together. I enjoyed the family life although at times, his guilt from the divorce made him a very soft parent.

There were times I felt the kids naturally took advantage of that. I nicknamed him ATM. He readily handed money over when his kids asked. Sometimes that led to us being shorthanded. We debated over the balance of it all and most times I won, but it became draining to debate all the time. Every time I felt that it was more important to teach the children life skills and life lessons, it was easier for the Prince to just let go and go with the flow. In my opinion, going with the flow doesn't help kids grow. As I look back, I realize he was also exhausted from his own battles and defeats in life. Maybe he didn't have the energy to put more discipline in place where it seemed needed. I felt teachable moments for kids are precious chances to guide them, and I saw it wasteful not to use them to help them learn.

The principals of life that build good people come from the day-to-day mundane skills that we all need to learn and do for ourselves. I loved (and still love) his children like they were my own. They felt like mine because I was so comfortable around them. They were typical kids, but they made me feel at ease and I felt that they loved me too. Although the teenager and I would have our struggles, it was typical and he grew into a solid young man during the two years I was in his life.

The two young ones were so easy to love and nurture because they were still in that "baby" phase, just in their tweens. I planned family vacations with them, special trips, made their birthdays memorable and all the special holidays too. All of the family occasions were so precious to me because I grew up without that for the most part and now I had my own family. I wanted them to be truly happy and I wanted everything to be memorable. I never had a birthday party growing up and family time was always strained and volatile.

The Prince and I often struggled over how to run our lives so that we could save and grow. He was used to spending money and I was frugal. I believe the basis of having a poor childhood made me cautious with money and made me work like a mad woman. My life experience taught me the value of money and I've always made the most of what I had.

Eventually, our thrifty lifestyle made it easy for him to pay down his debt. I found, like with many people, he convinced himself that he had a certain level of lifestyle to maintain. Similar to when he was married. In the end we agreed that it's easier and better to live within your means.

The Prince and I had many wonderful times together. We shared so many special moments with his children too. Time would pass and we all grew together as a family.

The sun did shine in that December for us both one week before his birthday and Christmas when holiday parties were in full swing. So much was going on and we had made it through a difficult first year together. On one cold night, we had come home from somewhere and were in our bedroom together talking. I don't remember the content of our discussion because what happened next overshadowed everything from that day.

I was turned around sitting on the bed. He went to his jewelry box and I had stood up to leave the room for something. The Prince turned around with a beautiful box in his hand and opened it and said, "What do you think about this?" I just looked at it and smiled and I couldn't help but think for a second, *Can you please ask me to marry you in another room? Perhaps not in the bedroom like my ex-husband had done three years before?* I was happy to see him standing there looking at me with so much love.

"I think you need to get down on one knee and ask me," I replied.

He stood there with the box.

Regardless of him being on one knee or not, I said yes. We were so happy. We were heading to a Christmas party that night that a good friend of ours was hosting. We agreed to not say anything and giggled, eager to see how long it would take before someone noticed the shiny bling on my finger. It didn't take long at all, and everyone reveled in how happy they were for us. They all knew how much we had been through and that this was a great celebration of moving forward to happier times. We were so in love and planned our wedding. We began even talking about the colors we would wear. We wanted it to be James Bond-like with a sexy and sophisticated feel to it. We agreed that Vegas would be our destination wedding.

The Prince and I had been together for just over a year when we travelled to one of my favorite spots in Quebec. St. Sauveur had long since become one of my favorite places to go to in the winter. I love to snowboard there and I loved the lifestyle and people. When I visit a cute little store I have always loved to shop at and pick something up. This one shop was loaded with Canadiana goods and rustic pieces. We picked out something nice there the year before for our home and there we were again browsing around. I had said to the Prince at that time, I love this place; I would love to have something like this for my own.

When we returned to home, we took a drive in downtown Belleville past some stores. I saw a few opening spots, but one in particular struck me as the *one*. With all the ins and outs of opening a store, I tackled the project with his support and encouragement. He worked on the store as a labor of love with his son. Hours upon hours we all worked to make the store take shape and it would be something that would always be with us. We breathed life into this venture and I was thrilled that I now had something to call my own.

The Prince had a new business that was beginning to move ahead with and he became busy investing himself in it. We pushed ahead together to make things work. The days became long between us. My work day finishes so early as a morning radio show host. I'm up every day at four o'clock and of course in bed every night at eight thirty or nine o'clock. My day is clear as of eleven each morning. I wanted to have some kind of purpose outside of the cooking, cleaning, meal prep, and regular life planning. I wanted to own my own business, a retail store, and to create success for myself as I had done for many other business people in the past. I was always able to make so much money for others and I love interacting with people, so this was a perfect fit. I envisioned our lives growing and the business, too.

It opened in March of 2015, while there were still further plans of construction happening in the downtown. This meant things would get ugly in the downtown core during the transformation of our district. Business went really well the first few months. I was so happy and relieved that my choice was a good one. Life was good.

Then, the construction started. Naturally, with the inconvenience, business slowed down to a point that only one or two people would come into the store daily. I found this decrease in traffic depressing. My heart sank, my spirit was being slowly quashed and I was so very sad, because my dream was being challenged by extraneous factors that were out of my control. For me, it would be like the idea of having a baby. You love the baby. To you, the baby is the best baby ever and you want people to see and love the baby too, but then, no one wants to come see it, because it is too difficult to get to it.

That's what happened with the store—my baby. Like most other business owners who suffered the same decline, I dug in. I worked so hard to make sure I was going to survive the wake of this disaster. For each month that passed by, the toll became greater on me. I worked long hours. I went from my mornings in my profession at the local radio station, to the gym, then to the store and at the end of the day, home. I was up and gone from five in the morning until six every night. By the time I got home every day, I was exhausted. In a bid to lighten my load, I brought in students from high school, college, and local programs to work at my store. I mentored them along the way in exchange for their help.

Physically and emotionally, I was exhausted from what was going on around me. My Prince noticed over time that I became withdrawn. Embarrassment got the best of me that things had become so challenging. I was distraught. That pending fear of failure once again loomed around and shrouded me like a dark storm cloud. When I got home each day, I just wanted to be left alone.

The energy I exuded from every demand in my life left me drained and unable to respond to the one person who needed me most. He wanted to be connected to me in some way. When I got home I often got ticked off about the state of disarray in the house. If the dog had soiled in the house, if the yard was not kept up, or the house chores were left for me to return to. Everything bothered me. Only when I really complained about it, did anyone start to help me. I silently resented myself for not being able to do it all. I resented him for not quickly hiring a maid to help us and although he offered that near the end, my frustration was beyond the point of return.

The catalyst for the end of our relationship played out with some very interesting and different perceptions on both our parts. He expressed my exhaustion and lack of desire to be with him intimately was selfish. He counted the days since we last slept together and that made me angry. He said how much things were not to his liking. Eventually, I took each request as another thing I didn't meet up to his expectations he had for me. This compiled with my own feelings of failing at the store, now I felt I was failing at my relationship too. By now, we all know I've been down this road before. The more he pushed me to open up, the more I retreated from him. I just wanted to cocoon in my pain. I couldn't talk to him, I was so upset with myself but I pushed on through every day. The more I persevered, the more tired I got. It became a vicious cycle.

By this point, we struggled along in our relationship daily. My emotional state of mind left me overwhelmed and enveloped by my own sadness. I was withdrawn and felt beaten down by the struggles of the store and life. One terrible night, he became so upset from my emotional withdrawal, the Prince couldn't take anymore. He demanded my engagement ring back and that I change my status on Facebook. I had avoided him for so long and didn't talk about my feelings.

When anyone tries to force a matter before I'm ready, I shut down. He wanted me to talk but I couldn't. I didn't know what to say. No one can make me do anything I don't want to do. I would cut my tongue out of my own mouth before anyone could make me speak if I didn't want to. That comes from being forced to do everything someone else wanted me to do. I endured that over the course of my horrific childhood. Now, when I'm faced with that kind of demand, it's like I get stuck in a certain gear. I can't seem to change when I'm provoked or angered. I go on autopilot, I see red. Some might call it stubborn. I call it survival. The fight or flight instinct kicks in, and there is no rhyme or reason to it.

What made it worse was the expectation of it all. The Prince used to go for long drives to clear his mind from time to time. Even though it would drive me crazy, he would go anyway and I never threatened to step out of the relationship because of it. I understood the need for time and space. His tantrum, as I call it, came late on a July evening and I had to work the next day. I arrived home after a visit to my girlfriend's house. With her, I was able to talk about how sad I was. I wanted to go to sleep. I told him I was going to sleep and climbed into our bed. Bitterness ensued, his response was one of frustration. He claimed the bed as his and said I couldn't sleep there.

Continuing the argument held no appeal for me. I went down to the spare bedroom, where I slept instead. I wanted to sleep and I didn't feel like talking when I was so hurt. He opened the door and demanded I take his ring off and give it back to him if I refused to talk to him. I told him repeatedly to leave me alone that I was going to sleep and didn't want to talk at all. I lay there on the bed face down and was near tears, but inside, my sadness morphed into a deep-seated anger. I insisted he leave me alone and go to bed.

"You've been drinking and I don't want to talk to you," I said. He continued to demand the ring back over and over again. I kept counting and thought if he asks one more time, I am going to give it back. I counted eight times and on the ninth time, something inside me finally snapped. I had such a rage of hurt rise up in me, that I took the ring off my finger and threw it at his head and told him to leave me alone.

"There you have it now! Go away!" My perception was he was trying to control me. The rage brought me back to that gruesome garage, where the villain controlled my every movement. Past the point of no return, I didn't want to talk even now, because I didn't want to break down. My lingering issues of my failed marriage came crashing to the surface. When he broke the engagement on me, I was devastated and angry. He used the one promise he gave me and took it away. I don't care what others do in life, but to someone like myself who has major trust issues, he had just signed his own death certificate and it became a slow and painful death I had to watch over the next few months through our last summer.

My heart splintered into a million pieces as I followed him down the hallway, wondering what he was going to do with the ring. He went to the very place where he took the ring out of to ask me to marry him months before and put it back in the box. As he turned around to look at me, the fragments of my shattered heart stabbed at me like a thousand knives, but profound sadness wasn't the immediate result. I turned to walk down the hallway and thought, *oh hell no! You did that. That's it. That's my reward for everything I endured, put back in a box and taken away from me.* I went and grabbed all my clothes and even the small dresser with my undergarments and dragged it down the hallway into the spare room. Desolation crowded and overtook me.

Things were falling apart around me and there was my Prince, piling the rubble on top of me. The weight of sorrow on my chest was so excruciating, I could barely breathe. In absence of any real rest, I got up to go to work the next day. The rage burning inside me in all honesty could have spontaneously erupted. It was so immense, I was sure the house would catch fire as I slammed the door behind me.

As the following few days passed, I shut down even more. He tried to speak to me and offered to give me the ring back. I refused, I would never wear that ring again. The damage was done. He broke his promise to me. The promise he would love me and that we would grow old together. We planned our wedding in Vegas and what we would wear. It was very real. We were in love.

Where was that love now? I was beside myself with grief and hurt. I had a wedding I was in that weekend. A close girlfriend of mine was getting married. Even though I was angry, plans for weddings are challenging to navigate through in the wake of a break up. I felt he would, and should still come. I didn't know how we were going to make it out of this one, but we agreed that he attend the wedding as planned. My sister and brother-in- law were invited as well. I booked a cool hotel for the four of us in Cobourg, the bride's hometown. It was about forty-five minutes from our city. I went the night before and he arrived the day of with my sister and brother-in-law. I made my way to the hotel, bought drinks and snacks for them to enjoy and continued with my bridesmaid duties for the day.

The wedding was beautiful and we had a lovely dinner too. It was all going well. The Prince had bought a new suit and he looked so handsome. The deep-rooted pain over what he did washed over me when I looked down at my own hand with no ring. There was my beautiful girlfriend marrying the man of her dreams. How do you swim through that kind of murky water on someone else's special day? The stinging inside my heart grew in leaps and bounds as the dinner and speeches moved into drinking and dancing.

That's when the tide shifted between our gazes from happy to sadness. I was happy for my girlfriend, but so annihilated over the crash and burn of my own fairytale ending. At the bar, we grabbed a drink together and we exchanged compliments. I remarked how sad it was that I didn't have my ring on. A part of my defenses lowered at that moment, I shared that he made things worse by taking the ring back after I had been upset about other things, too. I brought up the issue I had with a woman paying way too much attention to him at one of my parties weeks before. She was falling all over him and a few of my friends pointed it out. I was confident in my relationship and thought nothing of it at the time.

In hindsight she was clearly in pursuit of him and I should have known better. When that occurred, I had a party to hostess and couldn't make a scene. I also wasn't happy with him at that time anyway, so I let it go and turned my back on the situation.

Things were starting to piece together in my head though. He didn't like me bringing it all up, but I couldn't help myself. The memory of my ex-husband came rushing back and I thought, *Am I crazy?* The wheels came right off for a great many reasons and we ended up leaving the wedding early. On the way to the car, I was despondent, and crying inside. As all four of us got into our vehicle and headed back to the hotel, then came the actual crying.

To my detriment, the song that came on the radio as we drove was Blue Rodeo's hit; "It was Bad Timing," and then the tears really started to roll. Everyone was singing it in the car and I curled up in the corner and gazed out the window and cried. No one even noticed, for which I was thankful. I felt helpless and weak from my own tears, anger began to emerge to protect my pain. I asked to be dropped off to my car. I was sober, and I couldn't be around him anymore. My cousin lived in this town and I decided that I was going to go and sleep at her place. So, I left.

By the next morning, my anger and resentment overtook my grief. I decided when we got back I needed space in the house and I would be spending the rest of the summer apart from him. I was even more hurt now by his disregard for my emotions. The conclusion to our brief attempt to discuss where it all went wrong resulted with him sharing his thought that I should just take the ring back and not be so stubborn. Needless to say, it didn't help matters any.

Through the summer of being all over the place with each other, we struggled to repair the damage. It was difficult. I was hurt, he was hurt. We had major trust issues and we were in turmoil inside ourselves and our home life was strained.

I didn't want to come home, because I'd have to face all the things that were in front of us. In my mind, if I just stayed away, it was easier. I hoped my sadness would go away. We decided to go to therapy. This was a huge step where all the ugly past of my childhood and abuse came pouring out of my mouth. I thought before then, if I told him everything I had been through, he'd want to leave me and go away. I thought he'd find me unlovable if he knew what had been done to me by the villain. That part of a victim's shame is the hardest part of the past to shed, no matter how much you realize it's not your fault, you still carry guilt and humiliation over it.

Each week, we seemed to make some progress, although really small. It seemed miniscule if at all at times. We pushed through the summer into September. I finally broke down when my Prince said therapy wasn't helping us and that he didn't want to go together anymore.

The crushing blow came when he said I should just go on my own from now on. Abandonment struck yet again. The Prince told me something was wrong with me and he didn't want to be there to listen to anything anymore or resolve our issues between us. The truth in my mind is, if we had stuck to therapy a while longer, we very well could have eventually found a way to make it work. It would have taken time, but I'm sure we would have been able to. Instead, it ended.

Great, he bailed on me again. Our issues blew open when he took the ring away and broke his promise. Now he thought this wasn't helping just when I thought it was. The simple fact that he made an effort to gain my trust back and somehow mend what I was feeling inside, led me to believe that I would somehow forgive him and we would get back together.

During this process, I had stayed in the spare room and tried to find my way back to him. In the end, it didn't work. My next course of action was to take two weeks and go to a friend's house twenty minutes away. The peaceful serenity this place offered was what I needed now. We agreed I would stay a couple of weeks out there.

As it turned out, I instantly missed him. I was lonely. I texted him and called him while I was out there and he came out a few times to see me and we slept together too. Two weeks away was more than enough for me. My birthday was coming up and I wanted to be home with my family, so I came back.

Prior to my getaway I had packed up all my belongings in boxes. When I came back refreshed, I unpacked them all and I moved back into the bedroom with him. I tried to push forward. We both tried the best we could. We were careful with our words and actions. It was uncomfortable for both of us, I'm sure. I felt like a spooked horse being corralled back into the barn. My muscles were stiff as fear lingered through me and I knew how fragile my heart was.

From the time he took my ring back until right now, he had tried and tried to return it to me. This may sound cold, but I didn't want to wear it. It was tainted to me. The proposal was tainted and I had no idea how that could be repaired either. There we were in bed, the ring in the box on the dresser and all I could think of was *how the hell did we get here?* I just wanted us both to be happy, together. We had all these plans for our future, we bought this house, we made a life together and now it was all slipping out of our hands. When I look back, I can see there wasn't anything else we could do about it.

We couldn't resolve our issues. We tried and within a month they all resurfaced, and the pain had never really lifted for me. I still couldn't take the ring back. The memory of the moment he took it away was stuck on rewind in my mind, in the same room he had given it to me. I packed my stuff up once again and decided it was time to move out for good this time. I don't even know why or how we snapped again, but whatever wafer-thin link we had left broke beyond repair. My heart was still trampled, and no matter how hard I tried, I couldn't piece it back together again, even for the sake of saving us. My old instincts kicked in. Now I wanted to leave and run away.

We argued and traded insults and harsh words. Things became really unkind and I couldn't look at him anymore. My friends with a cabin offered me a place to stay temporarily until I figured out where to go and what to do. The Prince helped me move everything out of our house into a storage locker and even enlisted the help of his brother. We hugged good-bye and that was that....sort of.

I found out after the fact that the very same day he went out on a date with a girl who had a thing for him. It's strange what people do to try and distract themselves from the pain of the heart and I couldn't blame him.

We still kept in touch through texts and emails, but it was all insults and became a bit of a hurtful blame game. You did this, I did that...I swore I was sick of men and that I never ever wanted any man near me ever again. Guess what? You got it. A week later, a sweet young Buck galloped into my life. We met by chance and he said and did everything that made me feel better and he took away the pain in my heart. We had a lot in common. We had a variety of music we both liked. He loved arts and we had lots of common interests, and we hooked up as a result.

The Prince had told me when I left that the one thing that would end us forever would be if I slept with another man. The ultimatum made me so angry that when the chance came about, I did it anyway. It's unfair to get involved with anyone, sexually or otherwise while you're still reeling from a breakup, I realize that now. The new people that come along get the tangled web of split-ups. Despite intentions of distraction during heartbreak, it's using people as a Band-Aid to fix that gaping hole your heart. Maybe deep down inside, I made that choice because I didn't want to go back. I was mad as hell at him and my pain was immense. When I'm hurt, a switch flips inside me.

In under forty days of dating the young Buck, I knew it wasn't going to last, but he helped me avoid the brunt of the crushing pain from what had just happened. Truthfully, I thought I was ok, but I wasn't. Not really. Buck was an incredible person and he did nothing wrong in the grand scheme of things. He was perfect to me in every way; a gentleman, kind, considerate and compassionate, but there was no relieving the pain.

I reached out to the Prince a few times and chatted on the phone with him. I thought I was done with him. Done, done, and done! I was done, but old habits die hard. He was out doing his thing to try and forget me, so it seemed. It doesn't matter to me though, because I know in his heart, he did it even though he was still in love with me and I feel he was just trying to distract himself from thinking about me.

Speaking with him on the phone just solidified for me that too much had gone on for us to recover from. My Prince dove into another fully committed relationship quickly after me. To my knowledge, they're still together. Everything is as it is for a reason. I fully accepted it and went on with my life. Leaving the idea of what we once shared in the past was incredibly hard to do. We had a fairy tale, so I thought, but it was not meant to be.

It's unhealthy for anyone to get involved with someone just fresh out of a breakup, in my opinion. I see that now. When it does happen, it's called a rebound and a lot of us do it. It's a knee-jerk reaction to pain. It's never helped me, ever. I highly recommend not doing it.

There I was, alone again by choice and I needed to reflect on what happened over the course of the past few years. I looked at my ex-husband and my ex-fiancé and asked myself what I did wrong and why did I allow both of them in my life? I gathered some ideas about why and how I could still honor some of my reasons for choosing them and make a better choice the next time.

Both were in need of me, but neither knew it. I could see how I had the chance to be a loving partner and make their lives better. I knew it would take work and I felt the reward was the relationship with them. As a cathartic device, I poured more of myself into my writing, trying to get it all down on paper and reflect on everything.

As I look back, the man I saw as the Prince in my story, now seemed more of a Jester to me, because he acted like a fool with my heart. We were both fools. I tried reconciling with him and spoke on a few occasions. As it turned out, he made up his mind that he couldn't forgive me for my indiscretion, even though he had done much of the same. At this point it didn't matter who did what. We had struck a match and burned our house of love to the ground. It was all very tragic, because we had a lot of good times together, but in the end our bad outweighed our good.

Lucky in Love

So that was that. A few months after we split, he got engaged to someone else. Just when I thought his ability to hurt me more had fizzled out, I was wrong. Everyone makes their choices for their own reasons and you have to accept those reasons. Once he was my Prince Charming. The man I was going to rewrite my fairytale with and create a happy ending. Now he's the Jester who fooled with my heart and made me a fool to believe in love.

Chapter 10: FOR THE LOVE OF A BROTHER

When I moved to the big city, I had the heart of a small town girl, and I was pretty green when it came to dating anyone outside my ethnic group. Deep down, I always had an attraction to men with darker skin. When I was a little girl, I remember watching a movie called; *To Sir with Love one evening*. I fell in love with the debonair Sidney Poitier. Having grown up fairly isolated from the real world, there were very few people of any other culture outside of our typical small town where most folks were born and raised.

After I moved to Toronto, it became a feast of nations, and the islands too. My curiosity of different cultures grew even stronger. Throughout my time living in the city, I delved into dating on a whole new playing field. The possibilities of romantic interests were vast with new opportunities to explore. At one point, it had been close to ten years since I dated anyone who wasn't dark skinned. This wasn't a conscious choice. I drew a conclusion that once I was seen as open to dating someone of a different ethnicity, then others knew I was open-minded and approachable. To be clear, I don't care what color someone's skin is or what they look like. If you like them, then you like them and that's it.

I liked dating men of different cultures and I was intrigued by their ethnic foods, customs and accents. Nobody was the same. The first guy I ever connected with or kissed in Toronto worked in television and we became friends. Occasionally, we smooched and romanced one another, but never officially dated. That was because with our timing, one or both of us were always coming out or going into a relationship. I suspected in many instances, there was some overlap on his part, but I never asked. He was one of those people in your life that you're attracted to and you have a thing for each other, but not enough of a thing that would carry a relationship for any period of time, so it became a here and there thing. Casual at best.

Another guy I dated was a giant behemoth of a man, who worked as a bouncer at a club. One night while I was hanging out with my girlfriend, I bumped into him. Literally, as I passed by him I accidently bumped into him (wink,) and said to my girlfriend, "Whoa, is that guy BIG." He really was. A former college football player, this guy would later break my bed practically in two with his weight and size. That was a hilarious moment. It was short-lived when I found him to be a hot and cold kind of guy. I wasn't interested in adjusting the faucet for the entirety of a relationship. On the flip side, I would've had to buy some serious furniture to accommodate his physique.

Many of the guys I dated from different cultural backgrounds I met on the dance floor. I loved to dance, and still do. The dance floor was my favorite place to be. There's no set expectation of what someone needs to look like for me to dance with them. I danced with anyone who could dance. Several of the guys I chose to date caught my interest simply for the way they could move on the dance floor. Some moved the same under the sheets, but some really didn't.

For the record, in my personal experience, the longstanding myth that good dancers are equal with their sexual prowess is not necessarily true.

I could often be found at urban or reggae clubs. I loved the different music. So very different from where I grew up, where rock and country music was so popular. Beenie Man, Spragga Benz, Lady Saw and Barington Levy were all new names to me. Their music was so enjoyable. Like I said, I met lots of guys at these clubs and they were all so different. Not all guys were nice. Some were extreme players. I learned to play the dating game well from some of them. All races are the same, men and women alike. It doesn't matter.

There was a Chef I met at a club, when I was in my mid-twenties. We'll call him Handy. Outside of being a chef, I'm not sure what else he did on the side to bring in money. We'd been out a few times. Handy relentlessly pursued me to date him, and he had that all-too familiar agenda for his end goal. He saw me as a sexual object to covet. Sadly, I found him overly egotistical and greedy. Handy was visually beautiful. Long dreadlocks, almond colored eyes and he was quite the charmer with a unique accent. One thing I was sure of, was that I didn't trust him. Something just didn't sit right with me.

I spoke to a good friend of mine about it. I asked Handy to make a dinner that weekend and invite a friend of his over to introduce to my girlfriend. I thought having a nice double date would allow my good friend to get to know him better and get to know a guy at the same time. Not to forget that Handy was a Chef. When I think back, that's how he won me over in the first place.

Fast forward to the night of the dinner. The food and atmosphere was great around the dinner table. My girlfriend liked the friend Handy invited over. Not to the extent where she would ever see him again, but his company was enjoyable. After dinner, we had a little break before dessert and Handy gave a tour of his place to my girlfriend. He had a recording studio there where he produced music on the side.

Prior to my girlfriend arriving that night, I told her I felt he was shady and was probably hanging around other girls even though he denied it. On their tour of the house, I waited in the living room with his friend while we had a drink. It hadn't been more than five minutes when my girlfriend and Handy reappeared. The expression on her face was anything but pleasant. I got the sense she wanted to leave. We didn't stay for dessert. The once pleasant atmosphere of the evening had turned sour. I had a sinking feeling in my stomach, but I was already prepared for the worst. I hugged and kissed Handy goodbye. My gut told me it would be the last time I'd ever see him again. It was.

Once we got in my car, I asked her what was wrong. My girlfriend told me I was right to assume he was shady, because he tried to kiss her on the tour. I treated it with lighthearted humor. She asked if I was mad. I wasn't with her, not at all. Quite frankly I'd rather find out this way, from a trusted friend whose intentions were good, versus catching some other girl trying to kiss him. Less drama and still the same conclusion would be drawn—he was shady. End of story.

Dating different ethnicities was exciting for me, but I feel the need to proclaim: guys are guys, no matter who they are, what color their skin is or where they were born. There are about 196 countries in the world and I dipped into more than a few of them. Some of the exotic cultural backgrounds of men I dated were Guyanese, Jamaican, Dominican, Trinidadian, Antiguan, Bahamian, Grenadian, Ghanaian, and St. Lucian. In my time with them, I learned a lot about their cultures and discovered new likes for cuisine and other experiences they brought into my world. Regardless of heritage, my journey still led me to my conclusion that it doesn't matter where people are from. Some will love you immensely and some will play your heart like a song. Human nature is global, it's not limited to geography.

Chapter 11: THOSE WHO SHARED A NAME

There were some men in my past that shared the same given name. For anonymity's sake, I'll only reference them collectively as Those Who Shared a Single Name (TWSAN). This particular name they shared had a profound meaning that resonated with me. According to various sources, it means: *A healing*. A healing, is significant to me since, every of those TWSAN who came into my life came in when I least expected it, but when I needed healing the most. Sometimes, it isn't until you take time to look back on the reasons that you can better see why certain people have made their way into your life.

The Colin Farrell Look-a-Like (CFL)

I was in the middle of the fallout from my breakup with Junior, the acoustic drummer when I met CFL at a big motorcycle show in the middle of Toronto. I met him while he was browsing around with his father. He was tall, deep brown eyes and reminded me a lot of the actor Colin Farrell. This Portuguese/German guy was the perfect blend of subtle and sinful. My girlfriends and I were working the show, dressed in leather miniskirts and motorcycle jackets, strolling around too. We weren't hard to miss. Our eyes met and he couldn't stop staring. I noticed his dad chuckle at our mutual ogling. The four of us ladies in coordinating leather skirts, tank tops, jackets and boots, were attention-getters, but that was the point of the outfits for the event.

We plopped ourselves down for a break in the lunch area and not far behind us appeared CFL and his dad. They slowly strolled past us and CFL stared intently at me. I stared back. It's in my nature to maintain eye contact with someone who catches my attention. He smiled nervously in return, then glanced away. That was when I decided to get up and go over to him. My girlfriends kind of chuckled. By now, they knew me well enough that they could tell the hunt was on and my target was in sight. I laugh at how forward I am sometimes. He was sweet, and a little shy, which I found charming. We made small talk, his dad greeted me and moved on to the other booths while we talked. It was refreshing to talk to TWSAN, he had a gentleness about him and was incredibly polite. He gave me his number, we said our goodbyes and I went back to work with the girls.

I didn't call him that day. In fact, I looked at his number several times over the next few days trying to figure out how I would explain my living situation, because it was awkward to say the least. If a man wanted to date me at that time in my life, he'd have to pick me up at my ex-boyfriend's place. Eventually, I got over my worry and called him, and we went out for dinner. When he arrived, I went outside to meet him. My thinking was to explain my situation to him once we got out and connected.

Over dinner I explained the turn of events that happened with Junior (my drummer from the beat goes on chapter).CFL was very understanding. I shared how I was in the middle of moving out with my girlfriend. Until that was finalized, I had a month and a half remaining in this uncomfortable situation. CFL lived with his parents at the time we began dating, which didn't leave a lot of privacy. On the bright side, his family had a cottage about forty-five minutes north of the city and we ventured there a few times. There were a few opportune times he stayed at my place when my ex was away, but it wasn't ideal.

Sharing space with an ex when you're both dating other people can lead to some entertaining scenarios. Although I was selective about when I had company over to avoid crowding, I didn't always have the same courtesy returned to me. On one occasion, I returned earlier than expected and caught my ex bare-bottomed. He ran into the office area while the woman he was with grabbed a sheet and hit the floor. I wouldn't have seen this, except I had to pass through the kitchen to get something. The dining/living room area was all open concept. That was where he was sleeping since we split, while I stayed in the bedroom. It was a humorous sight to see, two people jump up and run for cover.

The trek up to a cottage, in the middle of winter with no running water was interesting, to say the least. The outdoor washroom was a cold and scary place in the middle of the night. It's a comical scenario where you have a new guy you're dating shine a flashlight outside in the middle of the night toward the washroom. This was instead of him escorting me there, because I didn't want him anywhere close to the bathroom. It makes it even more laughable when you insist he talk to you from the door so you can hear him. A romantic bonding moment, if you want to look at it that way, the two of us braving the cold so we could be together against the odds.

He was a sweet guy, but, as I got to know him, I became aware of some basic theories of living that I didn't like. For instance, he lived at home and drove an expensive car. It seemed a little over indulgent to me. If you have a lavish car, then you should be out on your own, from my point of view. His mother was an amazing person. So kind, giving and constantly doing for her family all the time. Many mothers do, but it was some of the simple ways that he could have helped his mother out in her day-to-day life that he didn't do. It made him seem spoiled or slightly selfish.

He never took out the recycling or garbage or helped around the house outside of keeping his room clean. If he didn't do these things in life now, when would he learn? When we lived together? I couldn't live with someone who didn't have the basic fundamentals of living and being an adult already in place. There was no way I had any desire to become any full grown man's mother. It weighed on me and when I finally brought it up to him, it was too late. Other things also played into existence, like the fact that he was in his late twenties and still ground his teeth. No one brought it to his attention and he never did anything to make it better. When I finally moved and shared a place with my girlfriend, he wanted to stay over.

The teeth grinding made getting a good night's sleep impossible. The grinding was relentless and drove me crazy, I finally put my foot down and told him if he didn't address the issue, he couldn't stay over anymore. Eventually, he got a mouth guard from his dentist, but by then I had so many other little things added up in my own head, on the "tally," that it was too little too late. The fact that he made some strange baby-like sounds when we were intimate together didn't give me an incentive to overlook the growing list of irritants. It was more like whimpering and that turned me right off...for good.

Breaking it off with him was hard. But like any relationship I've ended, I did it face-to-face and did my best to be kind and honest. When I look back on all the reasons I had to break it off with him, they seem kind of insignificant now. He was a great guy, but it wasn't the right time. My desire to spread my wings and fly outweighed the positives he had to offer. My career was my top priority and I grew tired of my radio gig in Toronto. At this point, it was time to explore other options.

Private Eye

Have you ever heard the song, "Private Eyes" by Hall & Oates? Whenever I do, I think of the private investigator I dated. I met this TWSAN at the gym. I'll call him PI. To be clear, it's always been my preference not to look up, make eye contact or socialize with anyone at the gym. It's my place of sanctuary where I focus on improving and maintaining my wellbeing. My devotion to my time at the gym is unwavering. When there, I focus on my workouts, and I rarely notice anyone else there. One of my best girlfriends told me that I was being a bit of a bitch, but I don't want to fraternize with the guys in the gym or project the idea that I'm there for anything else other than my work out.

This motto of work-out only, in turn actually appeared to intrigue more men than it managed to keep away. It would seem some guys use their local gyms as prime hunting grounds for a hook-up. A few guys made it their mission to seek me out in my space. They tried the testosterone-laced method of gaining attention by flexing in the mirror near me or following close behind each piece of equipment.

One day, I got caught in front of a piece of equipment that PI was headed toward. I looked up at him and apologized for getting in his way. I offered for him go ahead, but he insisted that I use it instead. So, I did. He used the machine after I finished, but not before he told me I inspired him by my dedication and focus. In reply, I suggested it helps to have headphones in and not look around to avoid distraction. He agreed. Against my own motto, contact had been made and now he knew my name. We chatted a little and he wanted to work out with me some time. Intrigued, I suggested the next day, and he accepted. Later, PI confessed to me he couldn't sleep at all that night, because he was worried I wouldn't show up.

PI bared a striking resemblance to Matt Damon; pretty cute and athletically inclined. He was witty and made me laugh. When I arrived at the gym, a little late, he had already begun to work out, and was ready to roll. At that time, I was really into Jillian Michaels, and I followed her high intensity workouts with weights. He held his own and kept his pace. I rewarded him with a trip to Starbucks, which turned out to be a first for him. I was shocked, *really? Never been to Starbucks ever?* I ordered for him, a Chai Latte, which I remember him most often order anytime we went there after that day.

In conversation, he never missed a beat and exuded confidence. A trait that struck me as impressive, he didn't seem intimidated by me. Later, he admitted he was, but, being a Private Eye, he was good at hiding things. During the typical discussion of where we were both at in our personal lives, he shared he was separated with two kids, and was still pretty broken hearted over his ex-wife leaving him for someone else not too long ago. In my experience, I've always found it harder on the guy when the woman leaves than the other way around. Male ego and self-worth crumble. From what I've been through and witnessed with my own circle of people, women tend to be more resilient when the man leaves first.

It's also harder on the next person with him after he's been broken. Because you're left picking up the pieces to put his heart back together. You can't help but feel that you're slightly the second pick, because his heart is still really with someone else. If you think about it like I do, he never planned on being with me, he planned on being with his wife, but she left and then he had to start over. Is it by choice or circumstance? When it is circumstance will they long for their partner indefinitely?

Eventually we all get over heartbreak, but some people take longer than others. There were times when I couldn't avoid the sounds of them arguing on the phone over their children. In a lot of ways, their relationship wasn't fully over because they had children. Parenting is a bond that doesn't disappear after the marriage is dissolved. There are now little human beings who need both parents, in whatever capacity they can have them. In most cases, that means communication, regardless of how good or bad it may be.

From the new girlfriend perspective, I couldn't be free from her and I never would be as long as I was with him. This relationship didn't just have two people in it, it came with the baggage of an ex that left me feeling he would never truly be mine. There was so much unresolved anger he had toward her, and himself. The reasons they split up were on equal ground between them. This dynamic stole the chance for me to feel special to him most of the time, and what girl doesn't need to feel special in a relationship? Already married with children, he had bought a house and was now separated. All things that I had yet to do or wanted to do.

He did include me in his family, we did fun things together and it was melding to some degree. His children were well-mannered and quite lovely to me. They were always welcoming and we got along famously. We never had a falling out during the whole time I was with PI. I lived on my own and he ended up back with his parents when he separated. His parents were also wonderful. They were kind, caring, welcoming and included me in everything. I really liked both his mother and father and felt like I was part of their family. We spent holiday time together and all kinds of dinners out and vacation time too. It seems workable despite the aftermath of divorce, doesn't it?

We were together over a year and a half and that was an accomplishment in itself. I say that because I had a pretty consistent six-month dating cut off with everyone else before. PI was a lot of fun, kind and the passion we shared made me swoon. Being a curious kind of guy, I know he had been to clubs with his ex and was an open minded person. We talked at different times about some of the intimate experiences that he had and I was interested in making him happy. He never pushed any ideas on me but he managed to arouse my curiosity. I'd never been to an adult club before and I went with him once. Only once. I wanted to know what went on in that kind of venue.

It was different, but not in a bad way. I was nervous to go, but not scared at all. For as far as the eye could see, there were topless people. Not many I considered attractive, but they were confident and comfortable with their bodies. We had a couple of drinks and observed more than participated in anything. It was more of an "investigative" trip and we never went back. The fact that we got along so well and rarely had any disagreements between us made me feel like we should go the next step and we decided to buy a house together. This seemed like a good thing to do as it would move him on into a new chapter of his life with me, in a new place and in a new space.

His ex wanted him to move closer to her for her convenience and the kids. Even though I liked her, loved the children too and wanted what was best for them, I just couldn't bring myself to make her life easier, when she had made mine difficult indirectly. Difficult by seeing and hearing them argue, fight and bicker over any decisions that needed to be made between them. They rarely got along and for the most part he tried to shield me from any of that.

The straw that broke the camel's back is when she didn't like the fact that he was moving on. I imagine part of her was hurt that we got our house together. I get it. She had moved on, but now that he was moving on, it was hard for her to take, even though she didn't want him back. Maybe it was the finality of it that took a toll on her. She tried to control the situation and shape it to her liking. She wanted us to move closer to her in her neighborhood.

Truth be told, I didn't want to be that close to her. I wanted my own space with him in my own house and where I wanted that house to be was my choice, not hers. She had her time with him and no one delegated where she bought a house the first time or the second when she lived on her own. This demand frustrated me to no end, enough that PI and I argued about it. I felt that she had moved to where she wanted to, so where we were moving should be our choice, and it was inappropriate for her to ask of anything from him.

Nonetheless, we compromised and found a place about thirty minutes from her, but not in her neighborhood. The day after we moved, it was hectic. I was busy unpacking and setting things up. I couldn't find him for a couple of hours. I learned later it was because she was crying and upset about the kids having a new place to live. She wanted to see him to talk and he went over to console her. I never knew about this until after we split up, but I knew something was already off with him. That dug a hole deeper already in my paper Mache heart. Deep down, I always knew he still loved her. Even though we bought a house together, it didn't seem to make a difference in his personal growth.

To be honest with myself now, I never gave him much time to settle into our house or the new life. The few months that followed after we moved were filled with some reservations and arguments about everything. My optimism lessened a little more each day about the likelihood of everything being ok. It got to a point I gave up and I wanted out. It became clear to me he would never be mine. I would never be special. It was too painful to know the partner I was trying to make a life with loved someone else and I felt secondary to her. For the most part, PI never intentionally made me feel that way. It was my own internal ramblings I couldn't shake.

At that stage in my life, I was still young and hadn't decided whether I wanted to have a baby or not. PI had a vasectomy and there was no option for us to have children, nor did he want anymore. *Where was my opportunity to be special* I thought? The moments that we had built up over almost two years started crumbling and slipping away. I wanted to leave. My internal suffocation grew each day, and eventually I left rather abruptly. He was devastated, which surprised me. I still shake my head a little at the thought of it. In my mind, if he loved me so much and was heartbroken over me leaving, then he should have considered his ex's feelings less and mine more.

A woman's intuition is powerful, and mine has never been wrong. Perhaps moments to feel special would have presented themselves with PI, and I would have settled in. Maybe it would've improved, but I just couldn't get rid of that sinking feeling it would never get better. There was something about the situation that seemed I would be settling with hopes of improvement. That's not how to find a happily ever after. That's how to make do and it felt terrible to give in when something didn't feel right.

Growing up as a child, I was made to feel insignificant by my stepfather, no matter how hard I tried. No matter how perfect I was, no matter how many A's I got in school or first place ribbons I won, I never was good enough. It's tough, but when I get that feeling at any time, it provokes my need to run and get as far away from that feeling as possible. My survival instinct kicks in, and I need to safeguard my emotions. No one can tear apart what I have pieced back together in my life and that's the one piece of control I can't relinquish to anyone, ever.

The quality of your life depends on the protection of your inner self and your beliefs, it relies on safeguarding who you are. I felt I had no choice. I never lived with anyone before with kids, and I was completely overwhelmed by everything. Money poured out of our accounts and it was tough on me. I worked all the time and we paid out a lot of cash for living expenses. I panicked thinking this is going to be our life.

The constant drain of money meant to me, we wouldn't have any to do anything with, ever. Finding out afterward that he went to see her because she was upset, made my heart hurt. We argued about everything leading up to the last day I was there. It was sad to leave the house and him when I saw how upset he was over it. It was also hurtful to leave his kids, too. I loved them and the split hurt them as much as it did us, especially his oldest. Their pain cut me deep. The trouble is, once I feel this way, there is no going back.

Flash-forward years later, I received an email from him. I never thought I would ever hear from him again. He said some hurtful and mean things to me in the end, but that's why they call it a break up, because something is broken. I've never had a hand shake departure and nice knowing you break up. Who does?

Years had passed and he reached out to me to have some questions answered and to see how I was. He learned of my marriage and divorce and always wondered if I was ok. I agreed to meet him for a coffee and chat a bit. Typically, I don't meet up with exes to rehash a relationship or the breakdown of it. This was something he needed, so I felt the least I could do is honor the request for coffee.

When we saw each other it was like no time passed at all, but the feeling that was there in the beginning when we first met was gone. This was more like seeing an old friend. We talked about where I was in my life now and how I was. He had a couple of failed relationships and wondered if he had been a good boyfriend to me. He had been. I explained to him how I felt and he told me that was never his intention to ever make me feel that way and he wished I had talked to him. He wished we had better communication on that topic and maybe things would have worked out differently.

Unfortunately, with the emotional scars I bare, communication is a touchy area. Once my internal alarm goes off and the safety of my heart is on the line, it's an automated response I have little control over. It's like that four-year-old in the garage takes hold of my senses. Fear and protection are the only things left at that point.

While time may not heal all wounds between him and his ex, they get along much better now. Neither of them had intentions of ever getting back together then or now and are much better off just as friends who have children together. But, that wasn't how it felt when we were together. There is a thin line between love and hate and there was a lot of hate between them then. It also served as a constant reminder that there was a lot of love between them at one point in time.

Lucky in Love

Sometimes you just get tired of looking at that reflection over and over again and you have to turn away to keep from going blind. We chatted about the past up to current events. I walked him to his vehicle, the same one he bought when we had broken up. I encouraged him to buy it, because he had a dad van when I met him, (I type this with tongue-in-cheek).We sat inside the non-dad mobile and decided it was probably best to just hug and give a kiss on the cheek. It was good to see him. He reached out a few times after that to check on me and to see how I was.

Once I was in Toronto when he texted me to see how I was and I told him I was near his parents' house. I asked if he had time for a tea, he was pretty busy, but agreed to see me real quick to say hi. Ironically, we met in the parking lot where we had originally met all those years ago at the gym. Just a quick chit-chat, because we both had plans. I sat in his vehicle once more and laughed at his funny jokes and his quick wit that drew me in the first time.

This time instead of just a hug, I was compelled to give him a kiss and see how it felt. It was nice. Different than before, because I tried to compare the beginning to now while I kissed him. A flood of thoughts came back on the many times we had kissed before. I had to be honest with myself, it wasn't the same magic of when we first met. My thoughts shifted to the logic that we'd been here before. I don't like to revisit old feelings very often, if at all. I have a motto, don't go backwards. Go forward. Quite often any issues you left unresolved will eventually resurface, even though time has passed. Perhaps feelings can change in a positive way, but my personal rule is to move forward.

Chapter12: FOR THE LOVE OF A BEAUTIFUL ACCENT

Accents are so exotic, and that appeals to me. When a man speaks with an accent, he sets himself apart from everyone else and people take notice. If it doesn't sound like the everyday language that you are accustomed to hearing, then why wouldn't it make you take notice?

Growing up in a small town, I didn't see or hear many people that were different. Another language makes you sound so worldly, it generates the idea you have pieces of a culture to offer that we aren't exposed to every day, and that is downright sexy. The sounds of an alluring accent spark my daydreams and interest takes hold. A man sounds so much more intelligent and appealing to me with an accent. French accents are romantic, English, too. If you speak another language you are almost guaranteed to get my attention in a crowded room no matter what your appearance. At the very least, I will talk to you, if only to listen to your words. Sadly, I have fallen for the allure of accents long before I knew what their words meant.

Karlof

After I began my transition to Toronto, freedom beckoned me. The need to get away and to grow into who I wanted to become was strong. I'm sure many people feel this way and I highly recommend spreading your wings in life. Try on different things for size to find a better fit for your life. During my time there, I took some Tae Kwon Do classes with the intention to become empowered and gain some of my inner strength back that had been stripped from me growing up.

In class, I was one of a very a few women. We were heavily dominated by men, and that triggered my sense of vulnerability. Although, as it turned out I really enjoyed sparring against the opposite sex. So much of my childhood I spent getting my ass kicked by someone twice my size and three times my weight. I admit, being lined up to men that were bigger than me was initially intimidating, but I quickly adapted and developed my confidence and my sparring skills. Not everyone in class was bigger than me. In fact, one guy was a little bit bigger than me and very intense.

At the time I was taking the class, I had just begun modeling in Toronto as well as having my first blush as a Toronto Sunshine Girl. A few of the guys in class had seen the photos, including Karlof. I often caught him looking at me in class, but when I did, he gave me what I perceived to be a dirty look and glanced away.

Initially this irritated me and I wondered what provoked the meanness. My ego was young and growing and I was used to men paying attention to me in a positive way, so his nasty looks bothered me. I said sarcastic things to him in jest and to tease him. Often we stretched out in class after the sessions. One day during stretches, he was in front of me and I commented on his flexibility. He practically scowled at me and I was intrigued by his disdain.

Weird, right? It's funny how that works sometimes, the more someone doesn't like you the more you wonder why and inevitably spend more time thinking about them. Reverse psychology maybe? I left the class close to summer after attaining my green belt. I was still commuting into Toronto for work and occasionally found myself with some time off.

One day I was in the town roaming around and visiting some stores. It was a nice day and I decided to visit the mall. I couldn't find a parking space close to the main entrance and ended up parking further away. I had to walk a bit and as I walked out of the parking lot toward the mall, I saw Karlof in the distance and we were going to pass each other on the sidewalk. I thought to myself, great, there's that guy that dislikes me in class.

As he drew closer, I found myself smiling timidly at him for fear that he would scowl as he usually did. He didn't. I said hi to him and he stopped. I was shocked. His medium length brown hair danced around in the breeze, his hair an indication of the grunge metal type music that was popular then. The look suited him. The intensity of his brown eyes was even more striking up close. In fact, my heart starting to palpitate. We exchanged pleasantries and he asked if I was coming back to class in September, My answer was no.

"So I guess I won't be seeing you there," I offered. The next words from his mouth, I wouldn't have imagined in a million years

"Then maybe we should grab a coffee sometime."

"Sometime," I remarked. "Why not now?"

Why not, I thought to myself. The sun was shining, I wasn't in town often, and here he was standing in front of me.

"Okay," he said.

We headed off to grab coffee. I was perplexed as to how this all transpired, but again, intrigued by the change in attitude toward me. Over coffee we had some small talk and found we had a lot in common. We both loved a variety of music. His tastes were a little different from mine, but it didn't matter.

During our conversation he shared he was from Germany and moved here when he was young. His parents opened a restaurant that served German cuisine. He spoke the language fluently and made the otherwise harsh language sound very soft and sweet when he spoke it.

I was impressed. We wrapped up our coffee, with an exchange of our phone numbers. At that time, there were no cell phones. When arrangements were made for a call, you had to be at your house to receive it.

We talked on a few occasions, each time lining up the next call. We quickly lined up our first get together; a date that would be one of the most romantic dates I've ever had. His parents owned a restaurant in town that wasn't open at that time. They weren't around often as they also worked in Toronto. He was alone most of the time and was finishing his last year of school.

To be clear, not college, high school. He was in grade thirteen at the time, and had told me he was nineteen. I was twenty-one. It wasn't a big deal really, but at the time I had no idea. It came up one night when a group of my friends were going to head out to a bar and I asked him if he would like to go. He obliged and I met him at his house. We talked as time ticked away, while we enjoyed a glass of wine together. His demeanor shifted, then he seemed nervous.

We finished our drink and as I took the last sip from my glass, he broke into a confession. He was not nineteen; he was eighteen and would not be nineteen for a few more months. I was taken back a bit at first, but it was only a few more months until he turned nineteen. When you're younger, three years seems a lot more of an age gap compared to late in life when ten years is a more significant amount to adjust to.

The first real date was incredibly memorable. Snow had fallen a bit on the night we had set for our date and the drive out to the restaurant was a little slippery. I was anxious already and the driving conditions made me feel it more so. I pulled into the driveway to a picturesque German-styled restaurant that had a small home beside it. It looked like I was in Germany with the new snow that had fallen on the roof top. I opened the front door to the restaurant and could hear a crackling fire roaring to the right of me. The room was aglow with a massive amount of candlelight, housed on a single table in the middle of a dark restaurant.

It was a breathtaking view I hadn't expected at all. I called out to see where Karlof was. His voice sounded from behind the wall from the kitchen. He told me to take a seat in the lounge area. The lounge had some hand-crafted wood furniture, no doubt shipped from Germany, with soft pelts of fur draped around them.

Crackles of wood snapped and popped from the roaring fireplace. Soon, Karlof emerged with a glass of wine for me and we sat in front of the fire and talked until the dinner had finished cooking. I was completely floored that he had gone to so much trouble. He escorted me into the fine dining area, where a table had been immaculately set for two. Candelabras glowed with dancing flames of lit candles. It was more than I had seen in my life at that moment. Karlof served me with constant attention. Our conversation floated all over the place. Including to the pending question I had as to why he had been so mean to me in class.

Karlof was very matter-of-fact about the why. He said he saw how other men reacted to me and he didn't want to be one of the guys falling around me. He felt he'd rather be no one to me than just one of the many. Wow! It worked, too. I found myself entranced by him, his charm, his class, and his kindness. I was absolutely smitten.

Soon after, love swooped in and took us both over. It was a heated love with tons of passion. He had respect for me and often demanded that I kept that respect in my focus when I worked in Toronto. While we were together, I was still modeling and doing work as a spokesmodel. I often did a variety of jobs through a reputable agency that would get work for girls for car shows and bar gigs. I found myself working a lot that following summer as a Budweiser girl. Karlof didn't care much for the direction my career was shifting in. He wasn't the jealous type, he just didn't like men leering at me. He found it disrespectful to the woman he loved.

For the most part we wouldn't talk about many of the gigs. He came to a few car shows that I was working and almost had a confrontation with someone once. Karlof had been talking to me on the floor of the show and another guy had approached me to talk to me and sloughed Karlof. The guy didn't think much of Karlof and I assumed he thought he was just another guy talking to me. There was a brief exchange of words. I was embarrassed. The nagging feeling like I was someone's possession didn't sit well with me. Karlof didn't like my modeling pursuits or anything that put me in the spotlight, and I was in the spotlight a lot with a variety of gigs.

At the time I was annoyed with what appeared to be jealousy to me. There was even a song on the radio at that time called, "Hey Jealousy" by the Gin Blossoms and it reminded me of him. In fact, that entire album played to the emotions of our relationship. I get it now. He was in love with me, and I was in love with him too--madly, in fact.

It was a relationship that I treasure to this day. At that time in my life, I was young and still in pursuit of who I was. I wasn't living in Toronto full-time yet, and was just getting a taste of freedom. The more Karlof pressured me about my job, the more I felt that he was trying to control me and where I was going. In hindsight he wasn't. The more attention I got, the more he was uncomfortable with it. We were so young and still delicate in our egos and confidence.

Toronto work kept me busy and I divided my time between the big city and the small town. I came back to see him on weekends when I had no work. I was blinded by my own emotions and fear of love. Over the course of the year that we dated, we split up three times and on the fourth time, it was the last and the end for me.

We had power struggles and differences of opinion on the type of work I was pursuing. After all, I had gone to college in that town to work as a Social Worker and he thought that was what I would be doing long-term. It turned out for a long while that I did more acting and hosting gigs than I worked as a Social Worker. Too many times, we split over the same things. All the beauty of our relationship faded. The perfect picnics in the middle of the woods, the dreamy hikes to the tops of hills that over looked the city, the dinners...we had wonderful times. The romance and all the love slipped away until there was nothing left.

On our final argument and split, he said if he ever saw me again he would spit in my face. He was so mad and so hurt. Weeks later, I received a letter. I had bought him a bottle of Calvin Klein Obsession as a gift for a birthday and when our relationship finally had ended, he dropped the letter off to one of my friend's houses, and the closing statement was, "I guess your love ran out just like the perfume you bought me." I was saddened by our split but the fear of being controlled ruled me. Not being able to achieve all the many things I had on my list of things to do overrode the love between us.

Our story ended, but I always felt bad about how we broke up and it stayed in the back of my mind. As time went on, I met others, some hurt my heart and some were hurt by me and nothing was really ever better or worse than his relationship with me. They were different people, but essentially, when relationships ended because of similar things, I would always think *what if...*

Fast forward to one day I was in my early thirties, I decided to reach out to Karlof and find him in the world. He moved back to Germany after he went to University and I searched his name on the net and found him. Go figure. He had an unusual name so it was fairly easy to locate him. I had some help with translating my letter to the email which went to his work. When he received the letter through his work email, he was on vacation with his wife and kids. A few days passed and he emailed me back, in English of course. I was in tears as I tried to apologize for the hurt I caused him. I've always felt bad about it. He was very forgiving considering the last thing he said to me was that if he ever saw me again he would spit in front of me.

That was how much he hated me and how much pain the breakup had caused him. So, to hear his voice on the other end of the telephone, all the way in Germany was overwhelming. We had a good conversation, we cleared the air so to speak and during our talk, he told me things were not going well in his marriage, but they struggled along. He told me he had two children, one boy and one girl. The day that his daughter was born, his wife had decided to give her a name which is very close to my name and when his wife told him the name, he immediately remembered me and smiled.

It was so good to hear about his life and that he had accomplished so much. He was even in business for himself. I wished him well and we said our goodbyes. It felt good to apologize and talk about what happened. I was happy to finally have all that off my chest. I didn't expect to rekindle anything with him, even though his soft voice reminded me of days and nights when I use to be so soothed by it. Had he wanted to rekindle things, maybe I would have taken a chance once again with him. He had a lot going on in his life at that time.

Bob from Emerald Isle

No, not the song, Bombs over Baghdad by B.O.B. That is the nickname I affectionately chose for an Irishmen I fell for. Things can change in a heartbeat. When you ask for change in your life, be careful, because it can happen. I never met anyone online before. It seemed shady. I was in my early thirties when online dating really started to become a real thing. I wasn't really into the dating online scene. I always had success in dating and never needed help but I was curious about this whole thing.

There was a website that was like a rate and date site before Tinder or any of that. You had to be rated onto the site to even be able to connect with others and the competitive edge was of course right up my alley. I liked the challenge.

At the time I was working as a radio traffic reporter, I had been for a few years and things had gotten a bit stagnant. I wanted to grow my broadcast experience into television and felt stuck. In times of restlessness, when I was off air, I checked out this site. I was juggling radio, modeling and spokes modeling, too. So, life was busy in Toronto and there was always something fun to do. It wasn't like life was boring. I just needed a change.

During my brief time on this site, I chatted with a few interesting people and met one that thoroughly intrigued me. He looked like Hugh Jackman and had an accent like Colin Farrell. For me, this was the ultimate combination of the two. He had a great job in Ireland and we chatted a lot over a few months. Bob was charming, romantic and so knowledgeable about a wide variety of topics. At times he struck me as a walking encyclopedia. Later, I learned he was very much a historian of the British Isles.

Over the course of about four months of talking on the phone and emails back and forth, my interest remained strong and I decided to take a chance by meeting him in person. He made his way to Canada for a visit. We hung out and went to different spots throughout the city to enjoy. Things progressed well and eventually I had to consider if this was ever going to work, one of us would have to move.

After some deliberation, we agreed it would be better for me to join him there. I took the ultimate leap of faith and headed there in pursuit of an adventure. I sold everything I owned and moved to Ireland. The idea of storing my belongings in a big locker held no appeal for me. A fresh start with nothing to hold me back, did. When I say I sold everything I owned, I mean everything. I sold my car and discarded old letters, cards and whatnot. I took specific mementos I still valued and packed up my life in two very big boxes that weighed about 150 pounds. With all my clothes in suitcases, I bought a ticket and left my life in Canada for a new voyage.

It was quite a quest. No, this relationship didn't last. I lived there for about seven months. During that time, I found that although we were compatible, something was amiss. While I lived in Ireland, I looked for work in my field of broadcasting, I did a little work now and then, but ultimately, I was a kept woman. It didn't sit well with me at all. He ventured to work every day and I busied myself around town. He knew I was a huge fan of the English cook, Nigella Lawson. To pass my time, I dug into some of my cookbooks and indulged in them as a new challenge. We lived in Athlone Ireland, weekdays tended to be quiet. I nicknamed it All Alone, because that is how I felt there.

It was even smaller than the tiny little town of Foxboro I grew up in. A few more shops, but quaint and small. Weekends we drove back to Cork, where it was much busier. That was where his mother and sister lived as well. Each day Bob would go to work, we picked out a recipe. My day consisted of finding my way to the little grocery store, picking up the ingredients and tackling the recipe. June Cleaver would have been proud of me, however, I never really fancied her. I found her too submissive and eager to wait upon her husband. However, there I was, being much the same way. I think week by week, I began to like myself less and less to the point that I had to leave because there was nothing left of me.

Every day was much the same, up early, go for a stroll, read the papers, shop, and cook, hit the gym when he returned, eat dinner and go to the pub. At first it's all so exciting. A new place, a new man and new prospects in my future. Bob spoke of marriage and had even talked about investing in a cafe for me. One much like Central Perk on the television show *Friends*. I loved music and we had ventured out to a few concerts while I was there, a rugby match and a Hurley match too. I did a little bit of everything while I was there.

Because of the proximity, I visited around Europe a bit and scooted across to England a few times. However, I couldn't envision myself being married to him. He was a devoted Catholic and to be honest, not very adventurous in the bedroom. Bob was a pretty traditional guy all around. I guess you have to trade off attributes here and there.

I can still remember the day I left from the airport in Shannon. This airport traditionally services the U.S. Military Officers, and they were everywhere that day. Bob drove me to the airport. The plan was for me to go home and think about the possibility of marriage and a long-term life in Ireland. Bob and I embraced, kissed and just before I got on the escalator to ascend to the departure location he said, "I feel like I am never going to see you again." I assured him that I needed to go back to Canada to think. I assured him everything would work out just fine and I would be back. In the long run, no, I didn't; go back. I consider myself lucky that he sent my belongings back. He was a good guy, just not the right guy. I later learned he married a lady from Spain and had two children. In the end, it all worked out for him.

OUI! OUI! – Mon Belle Copain (MBC)

While living in Toronto and working as a social worker now, I still did events and hosted. My schedule was busier than I had ever been. Living in the area of the beaches where you are surrounded by couples, dogs and babies, there wasn't a lot of opportunity to meet anyone. The fact that I was constantly working made it even harder.

Being in the entertainment and event industry, you always bump into other actors and models. If you're only ever surrounded by people in your profession, eventually you end up dating someone in it. There was this handsome male model...doesn't everyone want to date a model? It's the assumed ultimate possession right? The ultimate affirmation that you are dating someone who is "perfect."

If you ever do consider dating a model, be prepared to spend a lot of time on your own. If you're not into doing your own thing by yourself, then you might want to reconsider your choice. Who thinks about that stuff when you are struck by incredible, flawless features like height, and beauty? I was only twenty-three when I met MBC. We were set up together by a friend of mine who he was sharing his accommodations with. She thought he was the perfect guy. Not because he was perfect looking, but because he was such a genuine person on the inside, which matched his beauty outside. I have to say, after looking at his pictures she had shown me, he was pretty damn close to perfect in my eyes.

MBC called me on the phone to chat a few times and we arranged a day to meet. First dates are always memorable, right? I still remember the first time I ever met him. I shared a house with an older gentleman at that time. My housemate was like a big brother/dad to me even though his girlfriend was my age. He always looked out for me and offered advice when I asked for it. I told him about my pending date and I was a bit nervous leading up to it, so we chatted a few times about it. His advice was to just go into the date with an open mind and not to be too judgmental about his profession and just treat him like I would any other guy.

It was a beautiful summer's day on our first date. I peeked out the window while I waited for him to arrive, I wanted to see what he looked like in person. What someone looks like in pictures and in person can be very different. He pulled up in the driveway and parked. As he strutted up the steps, I drank in the marvelous view. He was about six-foot-one, dark wavy hair and green eyes to die for. Mind you, I didn't catch these exquisite details until I opened the door. To the naked eye, there wasn't a single flaw with MBC's appearance. He was even better in person than in pictures. We went on our date, he was well mannered, humorous, engaging, and intelligent. Did I mention he had a lovely French accent? Yeah, the accent.

There was one undesirable quality, I discovered. He smoked. Don't get me wrong, I quickly over looked this negative because in my mind, he was worth it. Aside from the health implications, the downside of dating a smoker is the lingering taste of tobacco on his lips. I'm not a fan of it, to be honest. MBC was an undeniably stunning man most women swooned for. Our connection was powerful, and we fell in love, of course, because as you've been reading, that's what I do. I fall right in love. It may seem strange to others, so many people feel it's impossible to find love, and for me, I've found it many times. I can't explain how it happens. It's like a magical door that glides open for me, and I walk through every time it appears.

MBC travelled a lot and was often in Japan and Europe. I remember the first time he had to leave for a few months and I thought my heart was going to split in two. MBC was booked to go and we planned a day of being a tourist in the city. We went all over and took tons of pictures. I printed many of them and filled my place with the memories of that day to keep me going in his absence.

Each day that passed was tough for me. It was hard for him to call, because cell phones were just being introduced to the world back then, so often he called from a land line and I had to be at home to get the call. I worked weird shifts at a group home, the shift work made connecting with him even more challenging. When we did talk, we spoke about his daily events, what was on the horizon and how much we missed each other.

My life seemed so empty in comparison. Each time I hung up the phone, my heart hurt. *Was this what the rest of my life would be like? Constant heartache?* I hated it. To ease the pain, I visited his parents a few times back in his home town and spent a couple of weekends with them. They were lovely people who embraced me when I first met them. They knew how much their son loved me and how much I missed him. They were so kind, but I wanted to see and feel MBC. He was so far away. I often received loving mementos through email from him to comfort and assure me. MBC was pretty romantic. He always looked for cute ways to say I love you, he even spelled I love you with all my socks out of my drawer and laid them out on my bed. That still makes me smile when I think of it.

One time, he was in the country while I was visiting my aunt in my hometown. He had to pass through so we planned to meet later on. By that time, he stayed with me in Toronto when he was in the country. It was Easter and we had to divide our time between our families, but he had something special for me. I was at my aunt's and he instructed me to not come outside to my car until after he left. I was bursting inside. I wanted to see him, but in a few days he would be home for a while, so I managed. Outside in the car was a giant stuffed rabbit strapped in the seatbelt in the driver's seat with a huge basket of chocolate in the passenger's seat. Swoon-worthy, right? He was absolutely wonderful.

MBC was unbelievable in lots of ways that I appreciated, but the loneliness between the times we saw each other killed me more often than not. When he was home, it was fantastic and he tried to immerse himself in my life as well. MBC signed onto the promotional agency I was with as a spokesperson. We worked a few jobs together including a fantastic party at Wayne Gretzky's restaurant where Bobby Orr was and the Great One, himself as well. We were dressed in sexy hockey gear and had to rollerblade around the place. Just one of the many fun things we did together.

One day, MBC was away again on a contract in Japan and we talked about the future and what would possibly happen. He admitted to me he had no idea what the future held for the two of us. He loved me and was committed to making it work. At that time, I didn't feel that was enough. The prospect of sitting at home during the best days of my life, waiting for a man to come home wasn't how I pictured my happily ever after. Even though MBC was kind, loving and wonderful in every way imaginable, he was away a lot, and didn't even know how much of his future I would be a part of.

When I look back now, I see my younger self as foolish and needy. I longed for a clear vision of my future with him. The unknown of where I stand in someone's life is a huge trigger for me. When I've committed to someone and ready to devote everything to them, how can I possibly give that when they don't know where we're going? I needed to know. I wanted him to say I was the one and that he saw something permanent in our future.

In retrospect, we were only in our early twenties and he travelled so much for work, he wanted to be sure he could provide for us both. Eventually, by phone one day, we ended it. It wasn't the last time we talked, though. After we split up, months passed and he eventually came back to Canada and sought me out. I had moved, yet he was persistent in finding where I had gone and wanted to talk. I remember it was late in the evening, I was walking toward my house and I could see something on my front porch. My cell phone rang and it was MBC. He asked me if I could see what was on the porch. I scouted along the street, looking for him and his car. He was nowhere in sight, but there on the porch was a giant bear with a bouquet of flowers sitting in front. I was shocked.

"Where are you?" I gasped. I stood on the porch and looked out to the street. To my surprise, there was MBC walking towards me with that intense, perfect smile lighting up his handsome face. My heart pounded with excitement. He caught me by surprise, something that doesn't happen often in my world. I had no idea what was going on or why he was here. He helped me with the bear and I grabbed the flowers and I invited him inside.

The confession he offered that night, was that he came to surprise me because he missed me terribly and wanted me to reconsider getting back together. Rehashing relationships I've walked away from is something I've made a point of not doing. I don't go backwards. It doesn't work for me. I have tried it before, but it doesn't work out. It hurt to tell him so. I wanted to take him back, he was so sincere. I wanted to believe him, and I wanted a future with him just a few months ago. In the end, his hesitation with actions and words made me doubt him and us. In my heart, I couldn't allow myself to go back again.

We sat on the couch and we negotiated, so-to-speak. We rehashed what had happened and how we could make it better. There was so much that he wanted to do differently. He was ready to take a break from modeling and perhaps work at his father's family business. I couldn't see him making that kind of sacrifice. "Why would you stop modeling," I asked? His career was something he loved so much, but he loved me more and wanted to make that sacrifice for us to be together. Fear spiked inside me. Deep down, I knew if I agreed, he would resent me sooner or later and we would fall apart again. I couldn't take that chance. Modeling careers are time-sensitive, it's not so easy to pick back up where you left off after the fact. Our moment had passed.

My life was in such disarray at that time. There was so much craziness going on around me. Part of me wondered if I should take him up on his offer and maybe settle down. Maybe it would have done me some good. I wasn't in the best place in my life and was working myself to the bone.

I can still see his face, and the sadness in his eyes before he hugged me goodbye. My heart crushed once more. I sat on the floor and looked at his giant bear, I hugged the flowers and cried. I cried for what was, and for the possibility of what could have been once more. I wondered how long he sat outside in his car. I debated running outside and down the street after him to grab him up in my arms. I wanted my legs to move, but they wouldn't. I wanted to take him back, but I couldn't. My self-imposed rule about moving forward and not going backward was a stumbling block for me this time. It never worked before for me. I did it once previous to meeting MBC and it almost cost me my life. You'll hear about that in the next chapter with a man I call Muzak.

Mon Belle Copain went on to his own happily ever after, eventually. I heard he took over his father's business in his hometown and married a girl from another country. Does that tell me I made the right decision? Would he have met her and fallen for her on one of his contracts even if I had taken him back? Or would that not have happened if I had taken him back? I don't know and I never will.

Chapter 13: MUSIC IS GOOD FOR THE SOUL BUT MUZAK IS NOT

Youth and naivety go hand-in-hand when falling in love with some men that are just no good. My most traumatic relationship, to my recollection, was with a young musician who was on the crest of good things. He was visiting from the States and living in the big city when I met him. One of my best friends and I decided to go out one night for a few drinks and picked a place that was fairly hip, but it was quiet that night. We sat and talked until we noticed two guys walk in. They were about the same height, and both showcased a lot of charisma. Immediately, one in particular drew my interest.

This guy had funky hair and had a strong presence I couldn't get past. They stood at the bar awhile. After a few flirtatious smiles and intense eye exchanges, they made their way over to our table. The one that caught my attention nestled in beside me, and his friend sat on my other side. We had some great conversation and laughs, before I had to excuse myself to the ladies' room.

Although the details seem unimportant, they really are to explain this guy. Muzak's bravado and boisterous behavior would be a challenge later on for me. I wasn't in the bathroom for more than a minute, when I heard the door open up and some heavy feet scuffled toward the stall I was in. To my shock and dismay, Muzak entered the stall beside me and looked over into mine asking me to hurry up. I yelled at him in as friendly a way as possible, considering how intrusive this was. I told him to get out. He laughed and hopped down and waited outside my stall.

How bold, I thought. I opened the door, walked over to the sink and began washing my hands slowly as I smiled. My nerves were unhinged. I dried my hands and that's when he pounced and pushed me up against the wall. Muzak kissed me so passionately, I thought he was going to devour my face. It was almost too much—almost. From what I later learned, too much was how he lived his life...too much of everything. Our relationship was intense from the first moment we met until the last time I ever saw his face.

In the beginning, our connection was fueled by fire for the most part. The things that happened between us over time, wore us down and tore us apart. Being a pretty talented guy, he was sought after by an impressive amount of various record labels and developed some great connections in the music industry. He toured with some big stars, but none of that mattered to him when his mother passed away unexpectedly. He had a lot of unresolved issues with his mother and it seemed right around that time his life imploded.

Muzak dabbled in drugs from time to time while we were together. When his mother passed away, he took it really hard and his drug use increased at an alarming rate. I watched the guy I knew fade away into someone I didn't recognize. Half the time he was around me, he was messed up on drugs, and or drunk. When he wasn't around me, I constantly worried about him and what he was doing. He'd call me in the middle of the night, messed up to come get him. Sometimes money went missing with no explanation.

There was nothing I could do, and then things shifted for the worst. He became aggressive toward me. On a couple of occasions, he had manic outbursts and physically grabbed me. During one situation, he got so aggressive I had to call the police to get him to leave. He took off, but he still called me every once in a while to try to apologize, or because he needed a place to crash. I always felt bad for him. I knew what it was like to have unresolved issues with one's mother; I lived with my issues every day. In response to my ability to understand where he was at, I empathized with him. That made me soft. That also made me vulnerable.

When I've felt empathy for guys I've dated, it's often become a trap for me to be in a relationship. My compassion and understanding for their situation left me to think I would want the same in return. Two wrongs can't make a right, as I've come to learn, time and time again. It's almost an error in human coding. You feel for someone's situation and you want to be a good person to them, but after all is said and done, you end up causing yourself more pain.

When you're emotionally unwell, I've discovered the best medicine is to be good to yourself and that doesn't always mean being good to others. You can't put yourself on the line all the time. But when I was younger I did and my boyfriends' problems became my opportunity to fix them.

Muzak had lots of problems with knowing himself and who he wanted to be. He also struggled with not wanting to do the real work to make his life goals come to fruition. Somewhere along the line, his ego made him believe he could have it all and everyone should give it to him, because he was a gifted musician and a creative soul. Creative souls shouldn't have to have real jobs right? Instead, he sponged off everyone and anyone he could, but from his perspective, I'm sure he never viewed it that way. Everyone tried to help him reach his career goals, but he never actually made it to where he wanted to be. He had some glimmers of success here and there, or so I've heard. Any brief shining moments of accomplishment seemed to be sprinkled with drugs, alcohol and drama.

After our relationship ended, he reached out every once in a while to bother me or to profess his love. He eventually ended up in jail for an assault of some sort, which got him a few months to slow down. During that time period, it was quiet in my life. I enjoyed the return of normalcy and everything was good. Just when I absorbed the calm, he got out of jail. Between the times Muzak's mother died and he got thrown in jail, his brother had reached out to me. He needed help to get the brother with special needs adjusted to life without his mom and living with Muzak. He asked me because of my experience as a social worker.

His brother proposed since he was on business most of the time, if I would move in for a while, help him get adjusted and implemented into the community, etc. It seemed like a feel good thing to do at the time. I wanted to help as I always have. With Muzak in jail, it felt safe and the plan was supposed to stay private. No one was to know. When Muzak got out of jail and prayed on the sympathies of his brother, he convinced him to let him stay for a couple of weeks. He begged his brother, and persuaded him once he'd gotten clean, that he only needed a place for a couple weeks. I was leery, but agreed to let him stay there.

Muzak arrived in good spirits and expressed his gratitude that I stepped up to help his family. He slept in a separate room while he stayed there, and everything seemed fairly cool between us. It was friendly. I felt mostly at ease, but still had my guard up. Addictions die hard, as I soon found out. The second week into his stay, his brother was out of town. I took his other brother to respite, as I always did on Friday nights for the weekend. I arrived back at the house to find it dark, except for a light on in Muzak's bedroom.

An eerie feeling washed over me at that point. As I entered the darkness, my stomach twisted in knots with angst. I called out to him to see where he was, and there was no answer. Figuring maybe he forgot to turn out the light before he left, I went about settling in for the night. I made myself a tea and headed up to my room and settled on my bed to read. The squeak of a door sounded down the hall, and then footsteps to my bedroom. Suddenly, he appeared at my door and I immediately recognized the dazed and glossy look in his eyes.

Muzak was strung out on something heavy. He began yelling at me, and accusing me of all kinds of things. My instincts told me to show a calm appearance, but my heart raced with fright. In my gut, I knew something bad was about to happen. That instant survival instinct to run in the opposite direction flooded me.

There was nowhere to run, though. I was trapped in the middle of the house, with Muzak in front of the only escape route. I stood up and tried to remain calm. He snapped and grabbed me by my hair and then my shirt. He dragged me in an intense struggle down the first flight of stairs into the living room. The entire time, I kicked and screamed as I tried to fight him off to get to the door.

There was no one next door. I knew if I got to it, I would need to run like hell. I was hurting from the struggle already. Muzak didn't give me a chance to get to the door. He dragged me down the stairs into the basement rec room. He screamed more at me about all kinds of things, it was all a blur. He dragged me across the cement floor and ripped all my clothes off my body, he climbed on top of me and he grabbed me around my throat. At that very moment, I thought I was going to die, I was sure he was going to kill me.

Terror pumped through my veins, but a strange calm filled me. My thoughts became crystal clear and extremely focused. From his rant and rave, he revealed this outburst had been fueled by a jealous rage over our time apart. His thoughts ran wild over who I had been with and who the men were.

Then he jumped up and said, "Tonight you're going to die, bitch. You are going to die." I lay on the floor, sharps stings spread across my back with the abrasions from being dragged across the cement floor. I was wounded, vulnerable and naked. Like a mad man, he stormed up the stairs. I could hear him in the kitchen. Paralyzed with fear on the floor, I couldn't force my body to get up and run for my life. Muzak returned with a knife. He grabbed a hold of me with one hand, braced the knife against my throat, and told me he should cut my throat open. He seethed with rage and said I was a whore that didn't deserve to live.

My fight or flight finally kicked in, I searched for a way out. Desperate to buy some time, I told him that I had been confused about my sexuality and that I was gay. I said I could never have loved him the way he wanted, because I was gay. It was enough of a confusing thought to him that it baffled him. His puzzled look encouraged me to keep talking. Stunned by my words, he moved the knife away from my neck and got off me. I grabbed my clothes and put them in front of me. I kept talking and reinforcing this thought to him. I softened my voice and he let me make my way to the stairs. I kept saying I was sorry and I just wanted to go to my room and forget this all happened. He allowed it, but followed me. There was still no way to escape without further provoking his rage.

My body trembled with fright. I scrambled back to my room and just lay on my bed. I never put my clothes back on, I just lay face down on the bed so that everything he did to my back was visible to him. I told him I just wanted to go to sleep and begged him to let me. I told him everything would be better in the morning. He left me alone, but I knew if I tried to sneak out, he'd catch me. It seemed like only a few hours until the sun gleamed through my window and I slowly put some clothes on. I still trembled inside. The house was silent as I made my way down to the kitchen to make myself a tea and see if I could get out of the house. Muzak was already up and in the kitchen. We had small talk about what he was doing that day and I calmly said I was just going to put last night in the past and carry on with my day. It would seem I was convincing in my performance. He believed me and left.

The moment he was gone, I ran up and grabbed a bunch of my clothes and took off to one of my best friend's houses. She assessed my injuries on my back. My face was scratched too, along with the bruises over my body that began to surface. Although I was reluctant, she supported me and insisted I go to the police. I was terrified of Muzak and just wanted him to leave me alone.

I did go to the police and filed charges. The next time I saw him was in court and when it was remanded, Muzak's brother begged me to back down from the charges of attempted murder and the list of assaults. He said he would leave Canada and never bother me again. I was terrified of him and I ended up perjuring myself in court out of fear. He was let go only to end up in jail again months later for an assault that happened in a bar. By that point, I had moved out and on with my life. I never wanted to see him again. The time with Muzak that was good was so overshadowed by the horrible things he did. I knew he would never come back from this.

The last time I heard anything about him, he got arrested in the States for the same thing that had happened to me. I felt sickened and ashamed for letting him get away with it with me and I hoped that the woman facing the exact same situation, had the bravery that failed me at the time. I hoped she had the courage to follow through and do the right thing.

That tragic chapter of my life made me leery again of men, and what the bad ones are capable of. I already knew all that from my childhood, and had felt like I failed myself again by letting someone into my life who hurt me. I had promised my inner child that would never happen again. However, love is blind. It blinds you every time to the truth about who they are versus who you want them to be. The lines can easily get blurred and when you are damaged by love's betrayals, you become susceptible to making bad choices. I have made a lot of bad choices, but I have also made a lot of good choices, too. Unfortunately, some of the good choices never had a chance because I was still dealing with the effects of what the bad choices did to my heart and soul. It's important to be still after a relationship ends to feel your pain, to heal your heart and to nourish your soul.

In hindsight, I wish I had followed through with the charges and had him put away. He ended up back in jail after that day anyway. Since then I learned that he also had a child and that he attacked the mother of his child in very much of the same way he did to me. He never learned and his anger and rage grew over time. I hope she doesn't fold like I did. I hope she did the right thing and stood up for herself. I'll never let it happen again in my life.

Chapter 14: TDH (TALL, DARK, AND HANDSOME)

"Tall, dark and handsome," is one of my favorite sayings. It's an old fashioned term that describes the epitome of the consummate male, or at least it is for those attracted to tall, dark and handsome men...but I digress. Being raised in an era where that term was widely used, it became engrained in my psyche. Whenever I meet a man, it still lingers in the back of my head. I was still young when I met TDH. It's when I lived in a big city. I just ran from another ideal relationship gone bad when I saw him in a mall.

It was the middle of the day, on my day off and I was browsing around. I stopped and leaned against the railing of the upper floor and glanced down at all the people passing by. With no set agenda for the day, I decided window shopping and people watching would fill my time. The air felt fresher, I was full of optimism and wide open to the possibilities of the day when I first set eyes on TDH. The moment I spotted him, it felt like time stood still and the air got very, very thin. As I looked up, he was walking down the corridor of shops toward me.

Everything seemed to move in slow motion. TDH strutted with a gait that reminded me of a thoroughbred moving through the field—striking and agile. Overwhelmed by his presence, I struggled to calm myself as he headed in my direction. After a few mutual glances back and forth, he passed by me. In a bid to seem casual, I leaned in on the railing in front of me, rolled to my left and took another look. Imagine my surprise when he stopped, turned and said hello. His voice was like butter—a rich, smooth butter that melted all over me.

We had an instant connection and chatted for bit. The details of the conversation escapes me as I try to remember back. One thing led to another, and we agreed to go for a coffee and get acquainted. Small talk ensued and we made arrangements to see each other again over lunch when time permitted. Although I didn't inquire much about his personal life, I didn't really care at that point. I was intoxicated by him and that feeling lingered for days until I saw him again.

We met at a restaurant that became our regular spot to dine in, over the course of knowing each other. It was always a busy place and I never once thought for a moment of anyone or anything when we were together. TDH was a compelling guy, but I can't explain to this day what it was about him. When I think about him as I write this, I wonder to myself; if I saw him today would I still be affected the same way? I love the quote from the movie Batman, when the Joker played by Jack Nicholson asks, "Ever dance with the devil in the pale moonlight?" That movie line perfectly describes the feeling I had for TDH. It was that dance between the two of us, the feeling of risky ambitions and not ever knowing what would become of us or what the reason was for the two of us meeting.

TDH made my knees weak at the very sight of him. I was always able to count on him to make me feel better, no matter what kind of day I had. His laugh was so infectious and his wit always tickled me. What I found interesting about this lover of mine, was the fact that I knew nothing of his life beyond work. I never asked, I never cared and there was always plenty to talk about in my life to keep our conversations busy.

We kept our connection fairly PG in the first few weeks we knew each other. Although that was a longtime when I think of what I felt when I first met him. When I saw him in the mall, I may have actually melted like butter. Knowing him was to enjoy our time together. I never asked about where "we" were going or what we "were," because I didn't care at that time.

Life was so busy and we saw each other when we could and kept in touch often. When we spent time together, he always made me feel special and I never had an ill feeling about him, ever. TDH was perfection; his smile, his laugh, his voice, his face, his body and most importantly, his mind. There was nothing wrong with him at all, but we just couldn't meet each other's yin with the other's yang when it came to timing, it was all off.

The dance of affection that occurred between us lasted a long time. Off and on I can't exactly remember. My brain said I should try to keep my distance from him, but the rest of me just got drawn back in to his energy any time I saw him. This went on for a few years and in between other boyfriends, he would surface, we would bump into each other or call each other to see how the other was doing.

During our time of lunches and romance, I fell for him. I couldn't resist TDH. I was young, impressionable, and impulsive. I was moved by my emotions, which I thought were right at the time. If the energy between us was so positive and charged, how could it be bad? We had amazing conversations, he was older, wiser and always had perspective for me on why the last relationship burnt out or fizzled. What I had done wrong in the relationship and what to look for next time. Part of me, as I look back, always felt that inside that the right one was right in front of me.

Lucky in Love

We always managed to drift in and out of each other's lives. As time went on, we eventually lost touch all together. He's a person I'll always remember fondly, despite the fact that he had been married. Yes, that little ditty, I left out. I knew we could never be anything based on the fact that I would never trust him. I knew he was capable of cheating and to what extent he could lie and hide the truth. I would never want to commit to someone like that. Once you know they can cheat, it's hard to believe they won't ever. There is a saying, "If they cheat with you, they will cheat on you." I refuse to waste my time trying to disprove that theory.

Chapter 15: REALITY CHECK

All through my twenties, and into my thirties, it became common knowledge with my friends that my dating patterns with any particular guy didn't tend to last any longer than six months maximum. I had it down to a science, but not because I tried to keep it to a set timeline. Through my journey to find true, lasting love, it seemed to be the ideal amount of time to discover if the person was worth continuing on with. I also found, it's a reasonable amount of time to develop a really good sense of who the person is as a whole.

Some guys didn't even make it to six months. Often, I sought out my friend's opinion of them if I was interested, but not 100 per cent sure. I'd invite him to their house or to dinner, and if my friends didn't view them in a favorable manner, they'd question how long we'd been dating. If it was close to the magic number and didn't see the connection being a good fit for me, they would say, "Well it's nice to meet you." They knew the drill, and they had a good sense of who would last in my life. Some of my close friends who were really outspoken would often come right out and say, "You know she usually dates guys for six months right?" We would all laugh, my nerves would rattle a little, but deep down, I got the affirmation I needed it was time to move on. Why get overly attached to someone who you are not 100 per cent sure about?

Lucky in Love

My friends grew to love the stories of all my failed relationships, and I became the love storyteller. Instead of a good horror story told around the campfire, I'd tell a story of a love that went up in flames instead. Often times I would tell the stories that were just absolutely ridiculous. Those gems got the most laughter, even at my expense. I often laughed at my bad luck, but sometimes I'd cry and ask myself *what's wrong with me?*

Why did I have such bad luck? Was it bad luck? Some friends offered insights that I sabotaged relationships on purpose, or chose guys who were all wrong for me. After the relationships crashed and burned, I dusted myself off, shook it off, and moved on without giving the last guy much thought. I pushed my feelings so far down and got rid of anything that reminded me of them and moved forward.

The feeling I was always left with in the aftermath of broken love, was that there was no sense trying to reminisce or have remorse over what could have been. *If it was meant to be, it would have worked out. Why bother looking backward,* I thought? That is my rule I set for my own life and I feel it's always for the better.

Here's the logic behind my rule; our perception of what was, what is and what could be, is skewed with the passing of time. It gets confusing. As soon as that relationship is done, it has changed you, and changed them. Scenarios have changed and you can't go back to what was, because it isn't anymore. It's not the same.

Everything has changed, just like the Taylor Swift song she did with Ed Sheeran. That experience has shaped you. The knowledge of that person has shaped your ideas, their behavior and yours mixed together has changed you. We can fall into a pattern of looking for someone similar or not at all, but in fact, it's an equation you can't solve, or else love would be so easy for everyone to find and keep.

You meet, fall in love and then live happily ever after, but that's not so for the greater population. Love is such a mystery and such an illusion. You can never quite figure it all out even when you are with someone who you are madly in love with. To over-analyze it could also mess it up, not paying enough attention to it can, too.

Therefore, when I look at all my relationships I've had and the times men have said it is my fault, it wasn't. What was my fault? Our calculation of who we were when we met?When you're spinning around in a cloud of hurt and pain, the best advice is to stand still and not make any sudden moves. Which is exactly what I didn't do or have ever done. I wasn't careful and I stepped forward when I should have stood still.

Nonetheless, it's still how my story evolves. There is no single book that can help navigate you through your life, because everyone's experiences are so different. Some may be similar in some ways and others maybe only a little. I feel we all look for the answers to our own questions and failures in other people's lives. I would like anyone who reads this book, to take a moment and be more forgiving of yourself and your choices.

Be kinder to yourself and to others. You can't make someone love you and you can't make yourself feel a certain way about them. Let go earlier when you want to hang on and maybe hang on tighter when you want to let go. Start living outside your comfort level. Start doing things that make you feel uncomfortable and you will grow.

In my experience, I've done all these things. I turned left when I thought I should turn right. I spoke out when I maybe knew I should be quiet. I stayed quiet and later regretted saying nothing. You have expectations of people, and they have them of you. No matter how much someone tells you not to have expectations, they linger around anyway. I've learned to accept what is and move on. I may be a warrior, but I'm not a fighter for someone's attention or affection. It's not in my chemical makeup. When you've been hurt so much by so many people in life, you learn to let go.

If it is meant to be, it will be. If someone is meant to be in your life they will circle back around and find their way to you. Everything is as it should be. It is perfectly imperfect, and that's ok. Don't rush through your journey. Every person you meet and every relationship you have is your experience and or lesson to learn. We will never have it all figured out, because life constantly changes and so do you. All of this is just fine. Let it be.

Chapter 16: POSEUR

When a wounded animal is in pain and hurting, the last thing it does is look for someone to comfort them. In fact, chances are, if you come too close to them, they'll bite you in a bid to protect themselves from the threat of harm. Often the animal will cower away from any kind of action and retreat to heal alone. Knowing this about survival instinct, I should have taken the action of a wounded animal after my last relationship broke off, but I didn't. I was in a daze of confusion, sadness, and pain and I walked straight into someone else's arms carrying that same amount of pain. Through this accident of sorts, I learned my greatest lesson of all.

Poseur is a man I went to high school with, saw on a regular basis at school, and even knew him by name, but never thought of dating him. I remember him clearly, because he was always so brooding and carried an appearance of being unhappy. This was so many years ago, but I remembered him. Years later, we'd both just left painful relationships that ended quickly. We were in very similar places though for very different reasons.

Once again, I had attracted an emotionally unavailable man, because I was emotionally unavailable too. I never considered that or acknowledged it myself, until it was too late. Loving an emotionally unavailable man is impossible. It wears on your soul, and in the end, brings you great sorrow. It's hard to watch someone in pain and be unable to do anything for them to make it better. It's even worse when you are experiencing the same kind of pain and trying to heal yourself emotionally, while someone is draining you of your last reserves.

Over the years, I tried to shake my desire to pick up stray dogs, lost puppies I call them, but more often than not, I find myself gravitate toward men who have been broken-hearted and broken down. Why? It's taken me this long to know why. Abandoned by my own mother, forgotten and unwanted, no matter what I did or didn't do, she never loved me or valued me for the person I was. She never wanted me, so my heart bleeds for those that are unwanted or neglected. I know how it feels inside to want that person you love, to love you back. I've stepped into this role more times than I care to admit, each time I hoped I could heal their pain and therefore heal my own. Subconsciously, I suppose, I've always hoped that righting the wrongs of others would help me heal as well. I also hoped that each time would be different from the last.

The definition of insanity is described as *doing the same thing over and over again, yet expecting a different result.* I guess I must be insane then, too. I prefer to call myself a "hopeless romantic," although others would call me a "love fool." It's entirely possible I'm that, too. The difference between the two I see, is when you're dealing with people, they're unpredictable. Everyone is different. I believe that everyone has the capability to change and grow.

To lose hope in others is to lose hope in yourself and your faith in humanity. That's something I refuse to do. I've never stopped believing. I've never stopped hoping. I barrel through life and I don't care what others think of me. Life is for the living, and while I'm living, I'll do as I please.

My biological father also abandoned me. He had impregnated two women at the same time in the same year, and had to choose between the boy and the girl. He chose to marry the woman who conceived a boy. He dismissed his own biological daughter, and for what? Because of my sex? I felt worthless when I found this out. My father didn't stop seeing my mother even though he married the other woman. He continued to visit me until I was four years old. All contact between us stopped when my mother started dating someone else–the villain.

I vividly remember his visits, and it often plays out in my dreams. My ability to remember something from the tender age of four baffles me. I suppose it's possible that it was so tragic for me, that it just became permanently etched in my mind. The last time I remember seeing my father as a child, he was a shadow in our family home. I remember screaming and yelling in the house and I felt profound fear.

My mother had been dating the villain. My father heard about him, and showed up at the family farm when he was there with my mother. My father had a pipe iron with him and I was later told that my stepfather had a broomstick to defend himself. My father wanted to kill him. My inner four-year-old wishes he had. He would have saved me ten years of an enormous amount of abuse and pain. Instead, he was forced out of the home and I never saw him again until I was eighteen years old.

Fast forward through my life and here I am again. I crossed the path of yet another man who is broken-hearted, hurt, and in pain. He was broken by his own choices, but underneath the pain, I saw a tiny glimmer of hope, or so I thought. You're shaped by your experiences and your choices. Whether you choose the good or the bad, you hopefully learn and grow from both. Poseur was in real pain, I later learned that it was because he was not living true to himself.

The amount of hours I spent listening to him rant and rave about his ex, or people who crossed his path day-to-day and angered him was overwhelming. I sometimes wanted to cry for his pain, but I couldn't allow myself to. I felt my own pain from my previous relationship and refused to let those tears fall. I completely understood where he was in his life and how he got there. I was grieving the loss of my own relationship and I knew he was too. We all make mistakes. Most of us learn from them, and some even grow from them. Others are doomed to repeat them over and over again. Some take accountability for their actions, but never change.

When I met Poseur, he wasn't in an ideal situation. For the first few weeks at the start of our relationship, things were tough. In fact, it got to a point where I honestly felt like I was drowning in his sorrow. That Sade song, "King of Sorrow," comes to mind when I think about him and where he was in his life. This was how I began to feel inside being around him.

When I couldn't take it anymore, I decided to stop dating him. I felt like he wasn't going to be able to move forward and I had to save my own self before my own pain resurfaced. More than a week passed before I saw him again.

During that brief time we were apart, I went out a couple of times with a man I had been talking to before I met Poseur. I hadn't moved forward with this man because I found myself still drawn to Poseur. We will call this man Fabulist because, that's a fancy word for liar. That was all he did to me; lie. He lied about not having a girlfriend. He lied about his status with this woman. He said that he had split up with this woman and that she contributed to the addictions he had previously. She was no good for him, he said. His family loathed her and he was done with her forever. He had asked her to leave his house and his life months previously because she was so bad for him.

There was a lot said about her and their relationship, and I believed him because I knew his family so well and had for most of my life. I never questioned a word he said because of this friendship I had with his family. This is why I was shocked and angry with him when I found out he lied about everything he said. I felt he took advantage of my trust. Trust that was not earned by him, but by his family and that made his actions toward me even more deplorable.

When everything surfaced and I found out from his girlfriend that he lied, she asked me about our connection, I lied. I lied to protect him even though he didn't deserve it. I lied and said our friendship was just that; friends. It really hadn't been much more than that anyway. However, I lied to protect him based on how long I had been friends with his family. He didn't deserve my protection and it was futile anyway. He was a liar to many for a long time and his lies eventually spilled out. In shock and serious disgust, I shook my head and walked away from the entire situation. *Not my circus, not my monkeys,* I thought. I walked away.

Unfortunately, I got lured back in by Poseur. I talked to him a few times after we stopped dating. I agreed to maintain a friendship with him as I felt he needed someone to talk to. I didn't want to abandon him entirely. I just couldn't be a potential lover and listen to him talk all the time about his previous relationship. It's anything but romantic to listen to. I did talk to him by text, and once or twice on the phone. It was a huge decline from every day, three to four times a day, when we first started talking to one another. He was still hurt and even though I was unsure about where he was really at emotionally, I felt bad for him. It was a tough place to be in and I felt bad leaving him with a bleeding heart.

At the time we parted, I simply couldn't stay because I absorbed all of his sadness and found myself becoming sad and depressed as a result. I still hurt from my own betrayal and broken heart. Poseur told me he missed me and appreciated the positive outlook I brought to his life. I listened. He wanted to see me and he said he was ready to move forward with his life. Unsure, I decided to take another chance and see him again anyway. I hoped that he valued his life more now and wanted to be the kind of man that I would want by my side.

I thought Poseur was given everything in life he ever wanted. He had a good mother and father, and I thought he would appreciate the same things I did. He ruined his happy ending, but I refuse to give up hope for mine. To give up hope is to surrender to those who have disappointed and hurt me, making me more like them and less like me, and that's not going to happen.

I have to stay true to the belief that real love exists and real love doesn't hurt you. In order to achieve change for a better outcome, you have to stop doing things the same way you did before. Truth be told, it's easier said than done, and can be incredibly uncomfortable to do.

Throughout the months that would unfold with Poseur, I couldn't let my real emotions show, I couldn't fall in love, I could utter the words, but I never felt them. He said those words most women wait to hear, but they fell on deaf ears and I wasn't able to return the gesture with sincerity. I wanted to love him beyond a friend, I hoped he could change, but he didn't.

He constantly flip-flopped back and forth from sadness to anger, all directed at his ex. He was so angry that she left him and that she wouldn't forgive him, and give him another chance after he had crushed her heart. He didn't deserve another chance, and even though she stood her ground, he still tormented her in any way he could. I felt bad for her too, because she would be stuck with him to a degree forever. You see, they had a child together. Their connection would be forever.

I tried to make Poseur's life happy. I was there for his children, and planned a couple of mini-vacations for his family. I tried to assimilate some sort of family vibe for him so he wouldn't dwell so much on the past. There would be moments of happiness for him, but then the dark cloud of his misery would blow in and cover the sun-shiny feeling I had created.

This happened over and over again for the months we dated. The tides of depression rolled in for me again. My mindset and the way I spoke shifted into negativity. I stayed focused on my store, my career and finishing this book. It didn't matter what I did for this guy, his unhappiness with himself and his life would ruin any attempt I made for us to move forward and find happiness.

At Christmas, I decorated, planned some activities like baking for the youngest child, and made a nice meal. I bought gifts for all the kids and the youngest of the three children stayed over on Christmas Eve. With all of this holiday spirit, I hoped he would be running on a high from all this positivity; but instead, he messaged his ex-wife early Christmas morning before any of us had woken up. He messaged her in a rage to let her know how mad he was that she never wished him a Merry Christmas. Who does that? To intentionally sabotage someone else's holiday because you can't let go of your resentment, it's cruel and seriously unhealthy.

That was the beginning of the end for me. I wondered how I would get out of this one. A few months later, we had plans to travel together and I knew that trip had been bought and paid for. I knew I'd be able to hang on for a few months, all the time I tried to make him happy at the expense of my own happiness. Even though I felt no love for him, my determination to make a difference in his life prevented me from the sane choice of stopping. I could accomplish anything I set my mind to, but love has always evaded me. It's never been a natural response for me; my natural response has always been to run when I have felt love. I never felt like running from Poseur, because I never felt love from him. Sure, he said the words, but I never felt them. I was stuck and I in return, became miserable and complacent. I didn't recognize myself anymore.

Most of my extra time was focused on finishing up this book. The final step was to let someone give it a once over, so I gave the final copy to a therapist I knew, Dr. Julie Gowthorpe, RSW. She regularly appears on our morning radio program and offers advice for better living. She's an author of a book I really enjoyed; *Tainted Love, Why Your Ex is Making You Miserable and What You Can do About it.* I gifted a copy of this book to Poseur, but he never opened it once. In hindsight, I now see that was because the roles were actually reversed. He was the one making his ex miserable.

I learned the value of love and family a long time ago when it was ripped from my fingertips at a very young age. It's precious and should never be taken for granted, nor should you do anything that will make it disappear, because it can and it will. I've seen it with my own eyes. However, the family life I grew up with was a horrible one. It isn't what I search for now as an adult. In fact, I ran from anything that remotely resembled what I grew up with.

All I've ever wanted in life was a good man, some beautiful children, and the loving family I never had as a child myself. I couldn't trust any of the men I met would stick around. I couldn't let myself believe in something I didn't know anything about. Now that I'm older, I've given up on the idea all together, and I wouldn't even think about starting a family at this stage in my life. I spent my life filling it up with so much to do, that I couldn't slow it down enough to devote the important time and sacrifice needed to raise a baby now. I spent my life acquiring friends to love me like family. I have girlfriends and guys who are only friends in my close-nit circle who are like brothers and sisters to me. I'm happy and feel content because of them all. They fill the void I spent so much of my life trying to fill. They are my chosen family.

Dr. J is a wonderful woman who I grew to trust and when I needed someone to peruse my book. I knew she would be the one to entrust it to. She read it through, gave me her opinion and then offered some reading material for me.

This was her *A-HA* moment about my life. As she read it, she realized I don't have bad luck, or poor judgement in character, and wasn't destined to be in unfulfilling relationships. She guided me to some online tests to try. After I completed a few of them, they revealed I had a diagnosable attachment disorder.

In fact, I've lived with it my whole life and had no idea. I found out that I was classified as an Anxious Avoidant. Most people who are Anxious Avoidant have grown up in a household with abuse and neglect. *Bingo!* That's me. I delved into some heavy reading about what this has done to me and my relationships. It was pretty complex. I'm attracted to people who affirm my thoughts and ideas about love and relationships. I'm attracted to people who trigger a pattern of feelings in me that often are not real and not good for me in my attempts to attain a healthy relationship, hence, my perpetual running. I read some amazing things by Jeb Kinnison at jebkinnison.com/bad-boyfriends-the-book/fearful-avoidant. This is an author who reveals a lot about attachment disorders and how to find a healthy and loving relationship.

The portion that struck home for me most spoke to the underlying fear and distrust of others. This author speaks to damaged self-esteem, how those afflicted want intimacy, but when in a relationship, the fear and mistrust comes crashing to the surface again and the survival instinct to withdraw kicks in. It describes cycles and patterns experienced by people with this type of attachment disorder. Reading this information opened my eyes to why the pangs of betrayal dug so deep for me, and why I'm so quick to reject others before they can reject, or crush me. Maybe that addresses my six month timelines in dating?

This author described how people afflicted with this type of attachment disorder have an endless dance of wanting closeness but needing to run from it the moment it approaches. It's a defense mechanism...*wait? That's what I've been doing?* This author outlined how these people tend to engage in a series of short relationships, ultimately finding faults in their partners, finding a reason to end it...to end it with these partners that get too close and suddenly become a threat to that person's emotional safety.

Hello? This author just described my entire dating existence. I love, I long for closeness, I find it, and I get spooked or triggered, and need to run away. It all makes so much sense now.

I spent my life circling these endless patterns. Perhaps deep inside, I knew something was wrong with the way I connected in relationships. I tried to communicate it to boyfriends in the past. I compared my feelings of being in a relationship, much like a wild horse running free. I enjoyed the freedom and security it brought me when I was able to count on myself and not rely on others who always let me down. But, on the cold days, the dark days of life, I long for that warm barn with food, shelter and maybe someone who loved me to stroke my mane.

Those cold days are the days I embarked in a relationship, tired from running, cold and lonely and I would want to be loved so badly, I got involved with people too quickly. Most men that met me loved my joyfulness, my love of adventure and zest for living.

Their new love appealed to me, but would soon suffocate me and I'd feel my freedom disappear. Stability scared the hell out of me, because it was so unfamiliar, no matter how hard I tried or how quickly I immersed myself in relationships, I always ended up running from those who tried to love me, or what I feared was a threat.

Time ticked past and it was spring again, just around the same time I met Poseur almost a year ago. I believe in luck, which is what I would call it when I had become enlightened and learned a lot more about Poseur then I wanted to.

I ended the relationship abruptly and for many, many accumulative reasons. I won't go into any of them or explain what I found out that made me end this once and for all. What I learned was shocking and I immediately turned off all forms of communication to protect myself. It's safe to say, I wish to never see or speak to Poseur again. He can go on and live his life in whatever way he sees fit and I'm happy to never look back. It's sad that I had to say goodbye to his children and his family because they were all lovely, but this was it for me.

This relationship cured me of my cycle. This last relationship drained me so much that I have nothing left to give anyone at this time. I need time for myself. I need space and I need to heal. I simply can't continue on this path anymore. Poseur is the last chapter in my Unlucky Love Life.

Epilogue: MY NEXT CHAPTER

Writing this book rescued me. The focus on it over the past year has allowed me finally to embark on my journey to heal and reflect on my own sadness. Now, I can avoid the use of false love to bandage my heart. The information I've learned during this process, opened my eyes and revealed the hidden darkness that drives me in my search for my happily ever after. It all makes so much sense now. I didn't choose to struggle in love. I didn't choose the wrong partners and fail. No one can secure a long-lasting, loving relationship when they had no idea they were living with an untreated attachment disorder.

Don't get me wrong. Just because there is an actual name for the challenges I've been battling uphill against, it doesn't mean I'll allow it to define me, or who I want to grow into. It means I'm now armed with two weapons I've never had before; knowledge and insight.

Now that this book is finished, my plan is to use it to reach other people who struggle with love and help them while I help myself.

While I continue to heal, I will rescue my inner child who's been scarred so deeply all these years. Before I can allow anyone close enough to love me the way I crave most, I'm going to reconstruct my self-love. That four-year-old needs a chance to have her voice finally heard, and this book is the microphone. She needs a chance for her deep-seated wounds to finally heal. I'm going to embrace that little girl from that horrible garage. I'm going to save her, because no one else ever did. Then I can finally allow myself to move forward into a healthy, loving relationship I won't get triggered to run away from.

You must be wondering how I plan to accomplish this tall order. Part of my self-reflection, I've realized I've never been single for more than two months in my entire dating life. My decision for healing is to stay single for a year in order to heal and grow.

Yes, I will date. I won't jump into any commitments with anybody. I'll take time to get to know a man with some casual dating before I ever get into another relationship again. I'm going back to the old school days of phone conversations, lunches, and casual coffees to get to know people better. Historically, I've spent more time deciding what groceries to get, or researching what type of car I should buy than I do deciding if a particular man is right for me or not.

Some people who have been hurt in similar ways to me have shunned love all together. Others have developed such fear and self-loathing, that they get stuck in a dark place and can't allow themselves to move forward. There are some who take that hurt, and twist it into a vengeful mission. With a goal to unleash their wrath on others, so they don't ever get hurt themselves again by trusting. On the other end of the spectrum, there are some much like me; die hard romantics that keep searching without a clue as to why they can't succeed.

Part of my self-healing has led to me sharing my story openly, as you've read earlier in my memoir. I've been a champion for youth through the Children's Aid, a poster girl, and an advocate for those in need of protection. I'm furthering this empowering role even now. Several advocacy and therapeutic agencies have approached me over the years. I've been invited to countless gatherings to speak to other survivors, and people considered vulnerable.

During these public appearances, I share my story in hopes my words will touch the hearts of others. So they hear there is hope, and that they can heal too. I want victims to discover they can have a voice, and more so, they can be heard and helped. I want them to find the strength they all possess, and see the endless possibilities that there can be great things in their lives. Those are my hopes and my dreams. Now, I'm making them come to fruition.

As for the rest of my personal journey and recovery, ladies and gentlemen, kindly stay tuned for the next chapter of my life. In a year's time, you can look forward to my next published book; ***365 Days Single—Confessions of a Serial Monogamist***. This time, how I approach my search for my happily ever after will be very different. What adventures do you imagine will lie ahead in the next year?

Made in the USA
Columbia, SC
18 April 2018